The Quilt of My Life

Writings by Joan M. O'Brien

Edited by Dr. Alyssa J. O'Brien

"Writing brings out the truth and allows you to love fully and to focus on that wisdom."

The Quilt of My Life

Writings by Joan M. O'Brien

Edited by Dr. Alyssa J. O'Brien

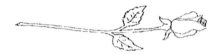

Published with love by Joan's family

Published with love by the family of Joan M. O'Brien.

EDITORS:
   Dr. Alyssa J. O'Brien
   Michael F. O'Brien

DESIGNER:
   Will J. O'Brien

TRANSCRIBERS:
   Sarah C. O'Brien
   Dr. Alyssa J. O'Brien
   Chris M. O'Brien
   Michael F. O'Brien

COVER:
   Original watercolor by Joan M. O'Brien
   Design by Will J. O'Brien

General inquiries should be directed to inquiries@joansquilt.org.

First paperback edition.

ISBN 978-0-557-62696-0

Visit www.joansquilt.org for a multimedia showcase of Joan's legacy.

CONTENTS

PREFACE

You, dear reader, are about to embark on a journey of written words. You may witness joy, doubt, faith, sorrow, pain, suffering, humor, acceptance, and love.

Novelist James Michener once said, "I love writing. I love the swirl and swing of words as they tangle with human emotions." This book, *The Quilt of My Life*, is a collection of Joan O'Brien's writings as she lived her last years battling breast cancer. This fourteen-year battle included nine surgeries, many multi-week chemotherapy and radiation sessions, doctor and hospital visits too numerous to count, and the devastating impact of extreme lymphedema and anasarca.

On May 18, 2009, Joan was advised that she only had a few weeks left to live. She went home where her family cared for her. As the cancer progressed, she fought and wrote and wrote until, nearly four months later, she passed on. Her legacy for her family, friends, and supporters is this book. Her words will swirl and evoke her emotions and yours.

Her daughter, Dr. Alyssa J. O'Brien, has gathered and edited her writings, her poems, and her journal entries into chapters about writing as healing, her memories of childhood, her poetry, her family, her professional life, her last days' journal entries, and her reflections in faith. No matter which chapter you read, you will be able to see a woman who, though suffering from a relentless disease, had grace beyond words and love for family and life. One of her hopes was that others who are suffering might find inspiration in her writings to pick up the pen as well, to find a writing workshop, and to write.

Many people are mentioned in Joan's writings, and she held in her heart many more who are not named in these pages; we offer a glossary of gratitude at the end of the book.

Michael O'Brien, August 2010

THE QUILT OF MY LIFE

I have heard that writing a memoir is like fashioning a patchwork quilt. I wonder what would be the pattern of my quilt. Would it be a crazy quilt, one with no particular pattern but expressed in fabrics of different textures and colors? How would I pictorialize the many years of my life and so many different experiences?

I start with childhood, growing up as an only child of loving parents— nurtured, sheltered, and spoiled by them. There were dancing lessons and voice lessons, recitals with many costumes, the uniforms in elementary school and high school, the involvement in the choir, the school plays, the excelling in academics. I did that for myself as well as for my parents, to make them proud of me. They were so proud. Going to college was a first in my family. No one graduated beyond high school. Bright, vivid colors come from the center of the quilt. But then dark, sadness, from the death of my mother when I was 19.

If people and places are each different colors, then my life as a graduate student, young wife, and mother would be a mosaic of every color imaginable. The thrill of learning, of being in the sciences, in chemistry and microbiology, a man's field where a woman could excel and achieve according to her drive and ability, and added to this being blessed by meeting my true love. What joy, how my heart beat and sang. Is all this really happening to me? Marriage while in graduate school, pursuing a Ph.D. in microbiology. First came love, then came marriage, then came Joan with a baby carriage ten months later. Deciding to finish my master's degree then stay with baby Christopher, more important to me than being Dr. Joan. Then followed the birth of three more wonderful children, living in France for eight years with so much travel, so many friends, so many rich and joyful experiences.

After the children were grown, although the youngest was still only 12, I went back to my career track. I was a law student spending every hour of the day studying. At the pinnacle of that triumph, I survived law school, and then came the biggest challenge of survival: a diagnosis of breast cancer.

It has been a journey of fourteen years, including many years cancer-free, enjoying my children, their accomplishments as well as their challenges and trials, and my success and fulfillment as an estate attorney, loving my clients and the stimulation of the work.

The quilt is still being assembled. It is not yet finished. I hope there are many years left. This section is muted, sometimes somber with bold patterns, jagged lines, overlapping dots representing current health challenges. I can look at the finished part of the quilt and find comfort and support as I continue to receive the same from my husband, children, family, and friends.

(March 3, 2009)

Joan painting a watercolor, June 2009

CHAPTER 1 –
"BUD OF A WRITER": WRITING AS HEALING

God Says Honey Yes Go

Writing with friends and sharing is a best medicine
I forget about aches, immobility, dependence of body
My mind is free to explore, to express, to appreciate
The words I write and the words I hear
There is always a blessing
The hand of God extending love in
Unexpected ways
My soul being purified
My body resting and refreshed
My heart open and soaring with love
Today, these moments are my divine gifts

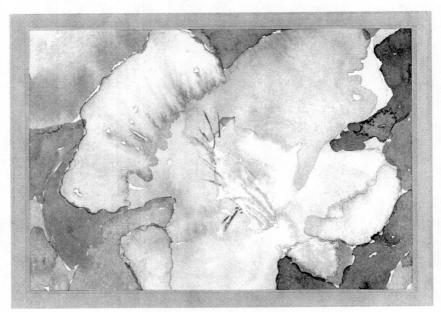

Original watercolor by Joan M. O'Brien, 2009

On Becoming a Writer

Throughout my life, I wrote letters, scientific articles, and legal briefs and letters. I never kept a diary or journal, wrote creative or personal pieces, or read or wrote poetry.

Upon my retirement from Blair & Potts, my daughter, Alyssa, very strongly and often encouraged me to write. She bought me Sharon Bray's book, *A Healing Journey: Writing Together Through Breast Cancer,* and Natalie Goldberg's book, *Writing Down the Bones: Freeing the Writer Within,* to encourage me. One Saturday, when we were attending Rita Trieger's yoga class at the Tully Center, in Stamford, Connecticut, Alyssa found a flyer advertising a writing group led by Drew Lamm. I started attending Thursday morning sessions at Drew's house and was hooked, although I only wrote at Drew's group. Since then I have started my own Healing through Writing group at the Bennett Cancer Center, in Stamford, Connecticut, which now comes to me at home. I plan to have Rachel Simon come and be my writing partner and perhaps Joan Petardi. I feel a need to write every day or twice a day. I write with my children, and we share our writings.

My writing has been a magic adventure. When I put pen to paper, I don't know what road it will lead me down. I can express my innermost thoughts, desires, fears, and strengths. The fears dissipate, especially when shared. The strengths are enforced. It is my vine to climb, to touch the sun and moon and stars. It is my staff of support.

It expresses me, who I am, so that my children and grandchildren will glimpse my heart and soul.

(July 7, 2009)

My First Experience of Writing

Sitting in a circle in Kripalu Yoga Center two years ago with Alyssa, Ken Nelson read various poems: by Rumi, by Mary Oliver. After he sensed he had us in a deeper, contemplative space, he told us to write whatever we wanted. I wrote a poem on gratitude. Being too shy to share it or perhaps not thinking it worthy, I didn't. Alyssa, reading it later, said, "It's beautiful, Mom." That was my launch.

Open Your Heart

I open my heart to love, mine and of others
I open my heart to acceptance of what is in myself and others
I open my heart to hope for myself and for others
Hope for the best life that is possible, framed in the
    acceptance of what is and can be now in the present
    and wrapped in a mantle of love, a gentle but all
    encompassing and consuming love
I open my heart to gratitude, grateful for life, love,
    acceptance, and hope.

(Written in Ken Nelson's class at Kripalu Yoga Center, April 20, 2008)

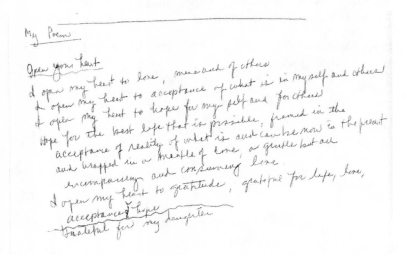

Arrival at the Fallen Leaf Lake Write Retreat

After taking a nap on Route 50, Alyssa driving, I awoke to the sway of the car. Opening my eyes, the grandeur of the scenery flooded all my senses. The brook was moving quickly, sparkling in the sunshine to my right. The majesty of the mountains, some still snow covered, embraced me. The majestic trees nestled in their stony soil. Then we reached Fallen Leaf Lake. The sun dappled the surface of the water which also reflected blue sky and puffy white clouds. Such a gift of a perfect day. Our world compressed driving down a narrow lane until we arrived at the Stanford Sierra Retreat at Fallen Leaf Lake.

We have adjoining rooms in the lodge: "A" for Alyssa and "B" for me. How good to be here with my daughter. Welcome to me, a bud of a writer. "B" for budding.

Arrival

Warm air
Blue skies and small puffy clouds
Majestic mountains
Winding down, down to the Lake that is Tahoe
A turn in the road
Narrow, winding, turning
Anticipation
Fulfillment exceeding expectation
This is arrival at Fallen Leaf Lake

Introduction session by Alyssa and Malena
Now write, write—that is why you are here
Arrival is always glorious

(May 7, 2009)

Writer's List of Places I've Left

1. I grew up in Bayonne, New Jersey, and lived there from birth until I entered graduate school at age 22. I commuted to college, over the Bayonne Bridge to the College of Notre Dame on Staten Island, New York. Finally, when I went to Rutgers University, Institute of Microbiology in New Brunswick, New Jersey, I cut the umbilical cord and lived at school. Not that I did not try the commute. I did for three months: two hours each way of highway driving. It became apparent that this was not a safe or wise way to proceed. When I made the break, what a relief to be away, in a center of learning surrounded by peers. Not that I was unhappy at home, but I was an only child, my mother had died while I was in college, and my father worked at night. Now a new world was opened to me, and I loved it. Although I came home in the summer, my heart was elsewhere, and two years after that initial departure, I married and left forever.

2. I lived in France for eight years. I became immersed in French culture —museums, exploration of different arrondissements in Paris, French writers, and most of all the beauty of the language. I lived in Versailles at first. The French were very friendly to Americans there. They invited us into their homes and for weekends to their places in Normandy, Burgundy, or Chantilly, places owned by the family for generations. These French were classy and compassionate. Although they could speak English, they insisted that French be spoken in their homes. When we played bridge on the weekends, it was played in French. I owe this extraordinary abundance of friends to my daughter, an adorable four-year old who attended the French école maternelle, who made friends with everyone, and who was soon speaking French as well as any native.

(January 15, 2009)

Writing for Sabina Beinstein on her Birthday

We have known each other since Alyssa and Paul were only a few months old. That is now a few months shy of 40 years.

I remember the day we met: Chris falling down the basement stairs, Gertrude Goldfinger taking care of Alyssa and you taking me and Chris to the pediatrician for stitches. That was the beginning of a long and very special friendship. When we moved away from Fanwood, New Jersey, we kept in touch and visited each other. Even when we lived in France, we saw you on our home leave, getting to know each other better. We were so busy with our growing families and now grown children and grandchildren, yet we always kept a unique place for each other in our hearts and thoughts—as close as family.

There have been many special celebrations, birthdays, weddings, bar mitzvahs and bat mitzvahs. Now it is your special celebration, your 70th birthday, and you are looking and feeling wonderful. The years from age 30 to age 70 have been so rich and rewarding for us. We celebrate now with you with love in our hearts.

(April 8, 2009)

Writing about Memories of Europe

My favorite spot anywhere in the world to sit with a cup of tea or coffee or a glass of wine always invokes in me memories of Europe. I lived in France for eight years, from 1972 to 1977 and from 1982 to 1985. Having an espresso in the afternoon or a Kir in the early evening at a café, preferably sitting outside, was an ingrained habit. When we moved back to the US, I certainly missed the ready availability of that trend.

In 2005, we went to Neuilly-sur-Seine, a suburb of Paris, with my husband, Michael, and my son and daughter-in-law, Will and Sarah, to one of my regular cafés, a busy café, with round formica-type tables rimmed in metal and high-back chairs with woven straw seats. We all had a Kir and watched the traffic go round and round the carrefour, horns incessantly honking, and fumes causing a constant pollution. At that time, the French still smoked in cafés, and we found we were offended by the smell and kept moving our seats. Somehow, the Kir tasted as good but the glamour was tarnished. I realized that I had evolved from the young person I was, and that my children being a different generation never quite experienced the same bohemian spirit of my youth. We had a good laugh over the noise, cigarette smoke, and the French as we walked to the metro to return to Paris.

(September 11, 2008)

Writing about Adventures in Shopping

In the early days of our second stay in Paris, in 1982, on many Sundays, we would travel by metro to an area of Paris called Clignancourt to walk through the Marché aux Puces, the world's largest flea market. Every imaginable thing and those you wouldn't imagine were on long tables displayed outside individual shops. There were miles and miles of alleys, circling each other so that you could easily get lost. Luckily, there was somewhat of an organization to all of this which was similar items for sale in the same areas. There were tables of buttons of every description, lace of every design, used clothing on hangers moving in the breeze like phantom images, and it continued for as far as you could see.

There were mirrors of every description: modern mirrors, ornate mirrors, mirrors removed from chateaus that were at least twenty feet high and ten feet wide, bronzes, plaster sculptures, silverware, pottery, fine china, linens, and antique furniture. Our mission was to look at and perhaps buy an antique. Of all the areas of furniture, my favorite one was called Biron, where eventually we came to know all the shopkeepers who would greet me warmly with my guests in tow for whom I served as French interpreter and price negotiator. "Voulez vous un verre de Champagne?" I was asked by a smiling shopkeeper, holding up a glass of the bubbly. The joy of the adventure was in the hunt as much as the conquest of the perfect piece at an acceptable price. In and out of many stores, perusing the furniture in each place. Carefully examining the wood, inhaling the aroma of rich furniture wax, and listening to stories of when the piece was made, so many dated back over 200 years, in what century, Parisian, Provençale, Burgundy, Normandy, and the story of how and why it was acquired when the grande dame died and the children could not agree which pieces to keep and which to sell and so they sold everything. "C'est dommage." The grande dame wanted the pieces to stay in the family.

I learned that the red marble on top of our commode, or bureau, was quarried only in the 18th century and then the quarry was closed. That fact, plus the carving and hardware on the piece, dates the bureau to be from the Regence period when France was governed by a regent until Louis IX was old enough to become king.

Another acquisition was a grandfather clock from Brittany: beautiful straight lines and warm wood, glass showcasing the ornate clock and weights. When we were returning to Connecticut, my husband bought our house in New Canaan—all trust on my part as I only saw the house in photos. I had him reassure me that there would be a place for this tall grandfather clock.

"No problem," he said. "There is a perfect spot in the entryway."

The perfect spot was immediately upon entering the front door. Luckily, it was on a lower level than the rest of the house. By taking off the door and hanging it to open in the other direction, the clock would fit. When I arrived in Connecticut and saw where the clock would be, I was amazed.

"What would you have done if the entryway was not a step down?" I asked.

"No problem," he answered, "I would have just sawed off the bottom of the legs of the clock."

Thankfully, the antique clock and the house work wonderfully together.

(April 30, 2009)

Writing about Place: Cedar Ledges

It has been many years since I visited Audrey Spellman's summer home on Lake Champlain named Cedar Ledges. As I drive along the winding road bordering the lake, I view the various bungalows on both sides of the road, some old and needing paint and repair, some newly remodeled. I drive up and park in front of Cedar Ledges. It was remodeled several years ago inside and out, so that I hardly remember the old structure. Once grey and weather worn, it is now cedar with red trim around each window: perky, fresh, and inviting. Three steps lead up to the front entrance covered by a peaked roof. Glancing to the left, I see the majestic lake and the steps and deck running from the back of the house down to the water, an expanse of water as far as I can see, to the horizon and beyond.

As I approach, Audrey opens the door, smiling brightly, and hugs me. It's so good to be here again. She invites me in. "You're just in time for lunch."

I smell bread warming and quiche baking. I see a big salad assembled and the table set with placemats, silverware, and glasses. We sit on the porch overlooking the lake and share all the recent events in our lives while tasting the spinach quiche, crusty French bread, crisp salad, and dry lemony Sauvignon Blanc. I hear the whisper of water caressing the deck and inviting me to come closer.

(May 8, 2009)

Writing about the Power of Place: Caneel Bay

When I meditate to Belleruth Naparstek's visualization and I am asked to visualize being in a place I love, I always think of Caneel Bay on St. John's. I have been to that resort twice, and both times were magical.

There are seven beaches with fine white sand. The topography at each small beach is different and ranges from very gentle at beach #1 to rolling waves at beach #7. What I love about Caneel Bay is the beauty, the peace, the tranquility, the attention of the staff to each guest, and the opportunity to walk out of your room a few feet onto the sand and then into the crystal clear, warm, and soothing water. Donning my flippers, mask, and snorkel, I let myself float forwards. Almost as soon as I look, I see beautiful bright colored fish, electric blue, startling bright yellow, luminous orange, some with stripes and dots, others solid in color. Some have diaphanous fins and tails that wave gently in the water. Some swim in multicolored groups, others in large schools, all of the species in different sizes, adults supervising their children. I kick my legs and move my arms and swim out further and further, deeper and deeper. At first, I pass low-lying displays of coral. The deeper I go, the higher the coral becomes, from houses to skyscrapers to mountains and caverns and valleys, all inhabited by fish, some very tiny, flitting so quickly, abruptly in their coral habitat.

Many times we visited one or more of the seven beaches, snorkeling in the water. We had high tea in the big manor house every day at 3 pm, had delicious meals in the four restaurants on the grounds, walked the trails, relaxed and read on the veranda or on a lounge chair on the sand directly in front of our rooms. We watched the red and golden sunset every evening and reveled in the clear, fresh, warm air and the sacredness of the place. There was no TV, no radio, no AC, just a ceiling fan, no room service, just the quiet unobtrusive attention of the staff refreshing our rooms several times a day and at night, turning down the bed, and leaving a different shell every night on each of our pillows. I always treasured the memory of the two visits to Caneel Bay for a week each, remembering the details as if I were there yesterday.

(July 19, 2009)

Writing about Place: Yoga at Half Moon Bay

On Thursday mornings, yoga is held at Enso, an inviting building on the edge of Francis Beach in Half Moon Bay, California. It is February 2009, and I am my daughter's guest and have been here several times before. I have met and spoken with most of the women who attend. We enter the anteroom, take off our shoes and enter the yoga studio. Everyone takes their favorite spot in the room. Ours is at the wall directly across from the windows overlooking the beach and ocean. Every time we stand, we will have a glimpse of the waves.

Women come in and say hello to each other while setting up their mats, blankets, bolsters, and blocks. We need these physical supports to ease us gently into the poses. To my left is Bonnie whose sons live in Asia and she has traveled extensively to visit them. Luckily, her daughter and grandchildren live stateside, not too far from her. Roslyn is across from me. She is one of the fearless friends of my daughter who dons her wetsuit and, along with my daughter and other friends, goes into that cold Pacific Ocean and balances on a surf board or rides a boogie board, catching as many waves as she can. They call themselves the

Wave Ho's. Marijane is at the wall across from Roslyn. She is my daughter's writing friend, a fellow author, and the head of the annual Women on Writing (WOW) conference. I met Marijane several years ago when I was sitting with my daughter in a café on the beach on a rainy day sipping my latte. Alyssa said, "I think that woman is head of the WOW conference."

"You have to introduce yourself," I said. She did and the rest is history. Alyssa is an integral part of WOW. My daughter is to my right and next to her is her good friend Deb. Deb lives on the next block from Alyssa, and they walk the mile to and from class together. I met Deb on her first visit to the class when she made an auspicious entrance by somehow sliding open the outside wall of the studio and entering that way rather than through the anteroom. These are just a few of the wonderful women in this class.

Courtney is our brilliant yoga teacher, a warm talented woman full of spirituality. I was here for Courtney's birthday when my daughter brought her a big bouquet of calla lilies from her garden, and we both signed her birthday card. The lilies always remind me of my mother as a bride 72 years ago, holding a bouquet of those beautiful flowers. Alyssa told me that Courtney had me in mind when she led the class that time. I believe it. It was slow but sustained, strong and powerful, with all my favorite poses—legs up the wall, twists, forward bends— and ending with a deep prolonged relaxation. Later, we all gathered, drank green tea, and wished Courtney "Happy Birthday."

Now I am in Half Moon Bay again. It is May, and it is Alyssa's birthday. I have contacted some of her friends to have a surprise birthday celebration after our class. This is my wonderful daughter, so full of love and caring who continues to enrich my life every day.

Now with her friends we can say, "Happy Birthday Alyssa," with all our love.

(May 14, 2009; read out loud by Joan to the yoga class at Enso)

Writing on Gifts from the Sea Revisited

Many years ago, I read Anne Morrow Lindberg's book, *Gifts from the Sea*. Her analogy of the stages of life to different shells she found along the shore was achingly beautiful in its wisdom and simplicity.

I met Anne Morrow Lindberg when I worked in an eye doctor's office in New Canaan, Connecticut. She lived in Darien and was the doctor's patient. Now she was elderly and a little forgetful, but definitely so charming. When I told her how I admired her book, she took it in stride. The praise was old hat, and I was definitely more impressed with her than she was with me.

But meeting Anne motivated me to give a copy of the book as a gift to my daughter. She also loved the book and it is a special bond between us—the fact that I shared with her something that was so important to me.

The ocean and its gifts have always had a fascination for me. When I was a young child, I vacationed in Atlantic City, New Jersey, with my parents. Those were the days of the Steel Pier, endless boardwalk, and no casinos—only the unending riding of the surf and waves. Many places at the New Jersey shore became familiar vacation spots: Avon and Spring Lake when I was in college and Long Beach Island when I was married with young children. Then our focus shifted to Cape Cod: Hyannis, Dennis, Chatham, and Orleans. In Orleans, we rented a house on Pleasant Bay with our children when they were young adults, recently married, and then with their children.

But there is one place by the water that always comes to mind when I listen to a meditation tape and it says, "Think of a place where you would like to be and picture yourself there." That place is Caneel Bay at St. John's in the Caribbean. It is a place of peace and quiet and beauty. I keep it in my mind and in my heart. The memory is of snorkeling in the early morning and greeting multicolored fish amid castles of coral. There is the taste of the salt and the buoyancy of the water, the vast blue sky and beauty of the gardens. I keep it in my heart and perhaps one day I may go there again, but perhaps not.

My lymphedema has made sitting in the sun unwise, and swimming is out of the question while in treatment. So there is a sadness in that.

But I do have the vivid memories which I keep alive. I recall Anne Morrow Lindberg's *Gifts from the Sea*, and the time she wrote that book was only a treasured memory to her in her later days.

I allow the time to pass and
   accept gracefully the shifting sands.
I look and see what is presently before me as
   this moment is now and then done.

(September 15, 2008)

Writing on Driving to Writing Group

The highlight of my week is coming to the writing group at Drew Lamm's house. I schedule my appointments, no matter how important, so that Thursday mornings are free. I can make it easily in 30 minutes, 25 with no traffic. Last week I set out in plenty of time and ran into a road closure at Nursery Road in New Canaan. Luckily, my GPS recalculated and brought me to Drew's, but through a much slower route and I was late. Today, I gave myself plenty of time knowing that parking might even be tighter on Drew's street because of an open house scheduled for the same time directly across the street.

I started my route and cautiously approached Nursery Road. It was open and newly paved. Great. On I went. I was going to be early and would have time to chat with Drew and the other writers before we started. Halfway down Raymond Street in Darien, a police car was blocking the road and all the cars were turning around and going back up Raymond Street. I turned around also, knowing that my GPS would find an alternate route.

Turn right on Red Rose Circle, it said. I did and guess what—back to Raymond Street. I turned around again and went up Raymond Street passing Red Rose Circle. My GPS, whose name is Gladys, then said to turn left on Old King's Highway and left on Tulip. Good, I thought. Gladys is giving me a different route. But at the end of Tulip there was Raymond Street, and the police car was still there.

On my third encounter, I stepped out of the car and walked over to the police car. The window opened and a policeman, who looked barely old enough to drive, asked if he could help me. "How do you get to Tokeneke Road?"

"I'm not sure," he said. "I don't live around here. But if you go up Raymond Street and turn right, that road should go through." That first right was Red Rose Circle, and I knew it didn't go through and told him so.

There was an open yellow truck parked in front of my car and a man in yellow slicker, yellow hard hat, and goggles approached the truck. He looked like he knew where he was. I ran across the street to ask him, "How do you get to Tokeneke Road?"

"I don't know," he said. "I'm not from around here. But maybe he knows."

I followed his gaze across the street to see a black SUV making the turn to go back up Raymond Street. The he was a woman, hair pulled back in a ponytail. We both asked her, "Do you know how to get to Tokeneke Road?"

She replied, "I'm going there now. Follow me. We'll go through Norwalk." Through Norwalk, I thought. I'll never get there. But I turned around and followed her. After a few rights and lefts Gladys stopped objecting and recalculating. I then knew I would eventually arrive at Drew's, and I did.

(November 14, 2008)

Writing from the Unconscious

I am afraid because I am having such trouble breathing. My chest heaves quickly in and out, with each breath a wheeze. Is it the altitude of Fallen Leaf Lake or more serious? I don't want to miss a workshop or event. Wisdom is necessary here. Alyssa, where are you? I need to go upstairs. This I realize—get some help, some oxygen.

What is the meaning and truth in what I am doing? Looking out at the beautiful lake, the mountains, the scenery, I am serene. Only inside I am agitated and afraid. Bring that serenity inside to me.

I think of a man who is old and wise and knows when to stop. What are the accidents of nature, the decisions we make that have an impact like ripples on a pond? The cause and effect is manifest in time, hopefully not too late and positively.

Let me go now to get help, my body cries.

(May 9, 2009; written at the Lake Tahoe Write Retreat)

Reflection on the Tahoe Retreat's Impact on my Writing

I learned so much at the Write Retreat. One thing is how important it is to write every day, and I am doing that. The retreat gave me tools: write from the depths, explore what you write and simplify, insert dialogue, a memoir is truth never fiction, which is making up facts. My poetry has become more refined, more from the heart. I remember the wonderful people I met and all their encouragement. The Tahoe Write Retreat was a wonderful experience for me in so many ways: the depth of learning, the quality of the instructors, the beauty of the area, and most of all sharing it with Alyssa. I am continuing to keep that spirit alive every day.

I sat at a picnic table overlooking Fallen Leaf Lake. The blue sky cloudless, the sun warm and caressing. The exercise was to write figuratively or literally to a phrase spoken by the instructor.

(July 17, 2009)

Writing on Happiness

I am gazing at water blossoms on lily pads, white, pink, ivory flowers—regal, calm, welcoming. It is lovely. It is peaceful. The light dapples through the leaves and shimmers on the water. I cross the arched wooden bridge and look at more ponds, more colors, more peace. I adjust my eyes and picture Monet's murals of his water lilies installed in the Jeu de Paume in Paris, France. But here is the real thing—don't miss it.

It is 2005, and I am in Giverny where Monet painted in the home he loved. To wrap myself in the mantle of beauty—this is happiness.

It is November, 2008, and I am sitting with my husband at the kitchen table. It had been raining rather heavily. Now, the rain has ceased and the sun appeared reflected in the drops on the leaves of the trees, on each blade of grass. Suddenly through the trees directly in front of us appeared a rainbow—large, distinct, overwhelmingly a gift from nature. I have seen many rainbows in the sky, but this one was here for us, right in front of us, amid our trees. We looked at each other and smiled. We even took a photo. How special it was to share that moment together.

It reminded me of another day when again we were sitting at the kitchen table and both looked out and saw a hummingbird. We had been trying to encourage hummingbirds to visit all summer by faithfully filling their feeder but did not see any until that day. A solitary green hummingbird gave us a show, taking a long time to peruse the flowers in my pots on the patio, and then took a long drink from the feeder. We were happy to share this little triumph together. These are the little events that make up happiness.

There are big events also—being with our children and grandchildren is a comfort and a distraction. I am thinking of that now, the moment, treasuring the little hand in mine, the hug and kiss and "I love you," the earnest talks and walks with children now grown who are loving friends and supporters. This is happiness.

There are the test results that are good. Clean CT scans, chemo working, continuing to survive and thrive. This is happiness.

Of all the goals set out and achieved, there are some that can't be attempted because of my cancer. My challenge is to work away those yearnings, to clean my soul and to even clean my closets to reflect the me who is now so I can savor these moments of happiness. These moments may pop up as crocuses do to surprise us when they appear suddenly on a barren lawn in the spring.

(November 3, 2008)

"Sometimes hope is knocked to the floor, breath knocked out. But hope rises, strong, glowing brightly."

Writing on the Sounds of Silence

Listening to "Mrs. Robinson" evokes memories of years ago: Dustin Hoffman and Ann Bancroft and a film shocking for its time about a woman seducing her son's friend. Certain songs recall past experiences. "Morning Has Broken" recalls Emmaus. I remember hearing the song again in the hotel in San Francisco when I stayed there for Sarah's becoming a Catholic. When I was younger, I loved classical music. Now I like New Age. Sometimes I prefer the sounds of silence. I do attune with the flute music and singing bowls Amy Zabin and Deb Pantolena present at their sound workshops.

I know music is known to be healing. Is it more healing than silence? If it is, why do I often prefer silence to music, or am I preferring silence to a certain type of music? I believe the latter is the answer. Silence allows me to be alone with my thoughts or to concentrate on what I am doing. Music transports me to another place—to sleep, to relaxation, to meditation. It helps me go inside and find my inner core, my center. When I am in bed, I hardly hear more than one song from my nature flute music before I am sound asleep. Perhaps I should actively listen to music more often, as now I am writing while Pandora is playing—it is not "unrelaxing" but does not have the same relaxing effect. I no longer listen to the high beat, intense music played at Kneaded Touch to encourage exercise. Some people run to high beat music to keep them going. Michael runs with no music. There is no right or wrong, just differences in preferences.

I, who loved music so much as a child, teen, and married woman, will embrace it actively once more. It may be a needed friend now, transporting me to new dimensions.

Let me fly on wings of imagination and dreams to a glory of bright light, to peace and calm, happiness and contentment, to healing.

(August 2, 2009)

Writing on Sound Healing

At the Bennett Cancer Center, in Stamford, Connecticut, every three months a program is offered called "Sound Healing." Amy Zabin plays the flute and vibrates large opaque white quartz crystal bowls called singing bowls. By circling a rubber wand along the edge a sound emerges, just a hum and then a loud sound that you can feel in your body. There are twelve bowls of different sizes from very small to very large. Not all twelve are used. Otherwise, there would be a cacophony of sound. If a bowl is filled with water and vibrated, you see herring bone patterns in the water. Extensive research in Germany, including electrical impulse tests, has shown that such vibrations are reflected in the water of our bodies and stimulate healing energy.

I am lying in a reclining chair in the atrium of the Bennett Cancer Center amid about twenty other people similarly reclined, all on a path of their journey, whether it be treatment or cure and survivorship. We take off our shoes, lie down, and close our eyes. We listen to the music and absorb the vibrations. Deb Pantalena comes around to each person several times, hits a special tuning fork and further enables a vibration on our bodies. Then she taps an instrument called an acutonic, a precision calibrated tuning fork, places it on the soles of our feet, and allows for another vibration. Relaxation is deep and complete.

Surrounded by the large plantings and trees in the atrium, looking up at the glass ceiling three stories high, I sigh deeply and close my eyes, thankful for this time of healing, and appreciative of the sharing of these two women who offer this program.

After an hour and a half, we slowly rise, file into the library, have some water and a snack, and share our experiences if we wish. I never want it to be over. I savor the memory and my body is hopefully continuing to vibrate with healing energy.

(August 3, 2009; submitted for publication to CURE magazine)

What Will You Do with Your One Wild and Precious Life?

I savor the 67 years of my one wild and precious life, and I am grateful for the many achievements, travel to foreign countries, and personal growth. Even my breast cancer diagnosis at age 52 influenced me to slow down, listen, go deep inside, and start to cultivate peace and eliminate worry, stress, and anxiety. On my personal list, my marriage of 43 years and my four children are my highest accomplishments, joys, and satisfaction.

In my intellectual and creative ledger, I am very proud of my profession as an attorney, my paintings, and now my writing. I can truly say I gave my best efforts to whatever was in front of me, whether it be reading a bedtime story to a child, painting a challenging scene, studying for a law exam, or meeting with clients. I can also truly say that I have no regrets and never look back.

The present phase of my one wild and precious life is more contemplative than active, although stretching, exercising, and walking must be part of the daily routine. Painting a watercolor is very fulfilling, very engrossing. I can tune out the world and just concentrate on the mix to obtain the needed color, diluting it to obtain the proper intensity and then brushing it on the thick paper, and watch the magic of color and form give life.

Finally, my writing is a wonderful outlet of expression for feelings and thought. I love writing with others and sharing our words afterwards.

My one wild and precious life has settled into quieter avenues, but still thriving and surviving and remembering that each moment of every day is important.

(July 6, 2009)

CHAPTER 2

"PORTRAITS FROM MEMORY": EARLY YEARS

"How has my character of today been shaped by my experience of yesterday?"

Where I'm From

Bayonne, New Jersey. A town of oil refineries and small town people where everyone knows everyone

Where nationalities are set up in orderly rows by streets: Italians, Irish, Jews, Blacks, Polish, Ukrainians

Where everyone kept their boundaries and respected each other unless the boundaries were threatened by dating or marriage outside the boundaries

Where memories of childhood winters were cold with crystalline icy sidewalks and streets, and snow drifts so much higher than my head that they looked like boulders

Catholic Education. Where in elementary school I wore a blue uniform with a white blouse, Peter Pan collar, white socks, and saddle shoes

Where the classroom walls were adorned with blackboards so high

Where the nuns wrote with white chalk which smudged their hands and black habits

Where my job was to erase those blackboards standing on a chair to reach the top, then wash them down every day with a large yellow sponge in a metal bucket of cold water

Where the local hangout was the drug store with its soda fountain of white marble top, and chairs with metal rims, backs shaped like a clover, and round seats

Where chores were part of daily life and scheduled weekly

Where every Friday evening I scrubbed the brown speckled linoleum kitchen floor on my knees with a bristle brush and rinsed it with a rag, dipped into water from a pail I pulled along beside me, all the while listening to the white plastic domed kitchen radio broadcast its weekly edition of "The Greatest Story Ever Told"

Holy Family Academy. Where my high school uniform was oak leaf green, A-line, loosely belted with beige long-sleeved blouse and Peter Pan collar, nylons, white socks, and laced shoes

Where my gym uniform was a gold tunic, gold pantaloons, and my name embroidered on the back

Where prowess in playing basketball was greatly admired

Where young women competed with each other and did not feel the threat or distraction of male competition

Where education was a key to success—to a scholarship, to college, to opportunities not otherwise afforded to those who were poor or lower middle class

Where you were the first one in your family to graduate from college and perhaps even from high school

Where education and reading led to thirst for more knowledge, for travel where the neighborhood gossip and small town provincialism seemed too suffocating

Where suddenly the world had to be bigger than my backyard

(September 18, 2008)

Joan as a child

Joan with her mother

Joan in Bayonne

Mother and Daughter

Being an only child, I was very close to my mother. I did not go to pre-school before kindergarten, so those days were spent with Mom. She did not drive. Consequently, we walked and did our errands. We walked to the bank to pay different bills: fuel, water, electricity. We walked to the grocer to buy vegetables for supper and to the chicken farm (at least a mile away) to pick out our chicken for dinner. I couldn't watch the head being snapped or the blood being drawn. I was fascinated, however, by how quickly the chicken was plucked of all its feathers and then heated over a burner with an open flame to singe away any remnants of feathers. The burning also produced the smell of burning flesh, which was uncomfortable to me.

We would walk back, chicken and groceries in hand, and Mom would start dinner. On the route was a nursery school, and I could see children running around, shouting and playing happily. My Mom said these children had to come to this nursery school because their mothers worked. I don't know if I felt sorry for them or for me. I certainly wanted company. A brother or sister would be nice, but I remember one sad miscarriage after the other. Play dates were arranged, often with the boy who lived on my street. It seems that he always came over to our house so my mother could keep an eye on us.

(October 2, 2008)

A Doll from my Childhood

When I was quite young, I think I might have been three or four, we lived on the second floor of a four-family house. I don't know exactly how many steps it took to ascend from ground level to the door of my home, but they were numerous to me, at least twenty, maybe more, and very steep. One day, I decided to walk down the stairs carrying my favorite doll. I can't remember her name, but it was something simple like Baby or Dolly, although now I refer to her as Savior. She seemed as tall as me with a stuffed body and plaster arms attached to the stuffing from the elbows on, and fat plaster legs attached to the stuffing from the knees on. Her face was plaster attached to the stuffed neck, with painted lips and eyebrows, a cute little nose, and the best part: her eyes opened and closed, and she had long eyelashes. Her hair was painted on her round plaster head. She was easy maintenance and large enough to fit well into my toddler clothes. I always had her wear a hat, white and frilly that tied under her chin. A long frilly white dress was my favorite outfit for her. So on that fateful day, I was carrying Dolly straight up like a baby with her arms around my neck, and I started down the stairs. Nightmare of nightmares, I missed the top step and started to plunge head first, holding Dolly in front of me. I was so scared because I knew that a three-foot high, one-foot thick metal heating radiator was at the bottom of these stairs. By some miracle, Dolly hit the radiator first, and I fell on Dolly. She saved me, and I have never forgotten that.

(September 11, 2008)

Early Years

When I started kindergarten and then elementary school, I walked to Our Lady Star of the Sea School several blocks away. I don't remember in what grade I graduated to walking with my friends, perhaps third or fourth grade. We made the trip to school, the walk home for lunch, then back to school, and finally back home at 3 pm.

After school was filled with dancing lessons and voice lessons and homework. Although I was in the high school reading group in school, I don't remember reading voraciously at home. I wish I had. It was a happy time, though. And I was the teacher's pet at school, which involved cleaning the blackboards.

(October 2, 2008)

The Inkwell

I remember being in second grade and sitting in the second desk of the second row of four rows, my designated place for the next three months. My wooden desk had a smooth top and a shelf underneath to store my textbooks, neatly covered in paper and marked with my name and the subject matter for instant identification. The desk legs were heavy metal and bolted to the floor as was the desk seat: flat wooden back, wooden seat, and metal legs bolted to the floor. The desk top had a groove for a writing instrument and a round hole for an inkwell. All students had the same set-up, sitting in uniform rows in our navy blue serge school uniforms.

A significant part of our curriculum was penmanship. I had a round glass container of blue black ink purchased at the stationary store, which I carefully lowered into the hole and gently unscrewed the top, being careful not to spill any ink. The writing implement was round, made of wood, and painted black with one end tapered and the other end flat with a ridge to insert the writing nib. I carefully inserted my nib into the holder, dipped it in the inkwell, and started to write.

What did I write? I wrote the letters of the alphabet, not stories. I wrote on my special writing tablet, with two solid lines an inch apart intersected by a dotted line exactly midway between the two solid lines. Capital letters had to touch the two solid lines, and small letters had to fit exactly between the bottom solid line and the dotted line. Just the right pressure had to be applied, otherwise the nib could scratch the paper or yield a large ink blot.

How has my character of today been shaped by my experience of yesterday?

(January 22, 2009)

Childhood Allowance

I was an only child, and I never had an allowance. I don't know why. It never came up, and I never asked for one. I know that my needs were well taken care of. Although my parents were by no means wealthy and lived simply, I had dancing lessons, nice clothes, toys, and was content. Perhaps my mother did not want me to frequent the soda shop, which I loved, or the penny candy containers. If I had an allowance, I would have bought a root beer float with a double scoop of vanilla ice cream, or a vanilla milkshake with chocolate syrup. I did have those treats once in a while. It was my parents' treat to me, and I savored it.

As an adolescent and young teen, I babysat and loved having my own money, which I diligently put away and saved until it was a significant amount, and I bought a record or clothes or went to the movies.

(September 11, 2008)

High School Memories

Last night, Alyssa, Michael and I watched the delightful movie, *The King and I*, with Yul Brenner and Deborah Kerr. The plot and song lyrics were very familiar to me, as I was in this play when I was a freshman in my high school, Holy Family Academy. I had a very minor part, one of the dancers, Topsy, in the Little House of Uncle Thomas entertainment scene. I was also one of the ladies dressed in formal wear in the banquet scene. Sister Anita James was the director of the school plays. She was a Josephite nun and wore a long black habit, black stockings and shoes, brown wooden rosary beads hanging from the waistband of her dress, a starched white round bib shaped like a semi circle covering her chest called a wimple, and a headpiece like a box on her hair with a white starched cloth over her forehead coming to a point at the top of a box in the shape of a triangle and covered by a black veil in black transparent lightweight nylon, draping over the top of the box, cascading to her shoulders and midway down her back. Even though so thoroughly covered, you could tell by her red eyebrows, freckles, and light blue eyes that she must be a fiery redhead, and her personality reflected this—a passionate, dramatic, and demanding figure. We spent hours in rehearsal, even with just a minor role, including nights and weekends. Once the performances started, we waited for our turn in classrooms, having our make-up applied and talking.

In sophomore year, I was a dancer in *Oklahoma*. Junior year *Annie Get Your Gun* was performed and *South Pacific* in senior year, but I was not in the play those years. I spent time on other activities, including debate team, dancing and singing lessons, and academics. I continued as the student conductor of the Glee Club for all four years, which I enjoyed very much. Every Christmas holiday period, we performed for the public at the Port of Authority in New York, lining up the stairs of one of the escalators, shut off for this purpose, with me at the bottom conducting. We all felt it was an important excursion.

Working hard on academics secured for me a scholarship to college, helped me in my competition for top ranking against Judy Padgorski and Alice Falkanski, two other super achievers. The awards for top in class and individual subjects were distributed among us. I remember being called several times to receive different awards during the graduation ceremonies, and my parents were just so proud.

The four years at Holy Family Academy passed by busily and happily. I had plenty of friends and did well. Since it was an all girls' school, make-up was prohibited, and we wore uniforms: sage olive green A-line tunics, belted in the middle, over beige long sleeve blouses with Peter Pan collars, wearing the required nylons, white socks, and brown and white saddle shoes. The question of what to wear or how I looked was never an issue. On the left side of our chest, we wore a patch saying HFA in large letters and color coded depending on our year in high school. We were as uniformly dressed as the nuns, all identically dressed in the same habit. Since in the late 1950's vocations were plentiful, over 95% of our teachers were nuns of all shapes and sentiments. Sister Regina stands out. She was the librarian, very thin, with a pleasant disposition, but with a strange idiosyncrasy. She cut out all the underwear ads from *Seventeen Magazine* before she put the magazine on the shelf for us to read. That often impeded reading an article to the end, to say the least.

So passed my high school years with happy memories for me.

(August 4, 2009)

Foods from My Childhood

My mother was the one who always cooked. I know that is the norm, but in my family my husband cooks and my sons cook and that is the norm.

My mother, Joan Meehan, being of Ukrainian heritage (actually born in Kiev in the Ukraine), gave her food a Slavic flavor. One of my favorites was kielbasa cooked in sauerkraut, Mom style. She sautéed onion with the sauerkraut, then added tomato puree (the secret ingredient) and the kielbasa. I believe the kielbasa was parboiled first then cut into two-inch pieces and added to the rest.

Cooking slowly in an oval heavy metal casserole with solid glass lid (it whetted the appetite), yielded sensory and visionary delights. I could barely wait to sit at the kitchen table covered with the blue and red oil cloth tablecloth and be served this delight together with boiled potatoes and rye bread. Sometimes hotdogs cut into two-inch slices were substituted for the kielbasa. I could never get enough.

One day I did have too much and was sick. There can be t[c] good thing. After that I was less enamored but reflect on the n... recalling the smell and the taste with great fondness.

Holiday time, especially Easter, was a flurry of flour and activity. Homemade pierogi and homemade bread, babka, were prepared. For the pierogi, the flour was mixed with egg and water in a well in the middle. Once mixed it was chilled then rolled out and cut into circles on a big sheet. Each half of the circle was filled with a heaping tablespoon of either cooked potato and cheese or cooked sauerkraut, then folded over the ends pricked together. They were carefully cooked in a large pot of boiling water and, when done, laid out to cool. When ready to be served, they were sautéed in butter and onion, with sour cream on the side.

The making of babka was a more time-consuming project, sprinkling yeast over warm water, adding flour and eggs, probably some other ingredients. Often golden raisins were added. The flour was kneaded, left to rise, punched down, and kneaded again.

Shaped into loaves and finally ready to bake, a cross was carefully placed on the top of each loaf and then all was coated in an egg wash to give the beautiful brown glow. There was also homemade horseradish, red from the addition of fresh beets, along with kielbasa and herring.

Easter Saturday, a display was set on the large coffee table in the living room: white cloth, candles, and the food. I heard a knock and lit the candles. Twinkling hall bells announced the arrival of the Ukrainian priest, in full traditional robes, who had come to bless our food.

(April 16, 2009)

By My Clothes You Shall Know Me

When I remember certain periods in my life, I often think of the clothes I wore at that time. There is an apparel association with doing things, going places, and meeting people.

I recall an Easter in my pre-adolescent years wearing a very large brimmed straw hat adorned with fruit, not plastic fruit but solid, heavy-duty plaster fruit shaped and shellacked. There were big cherries and blackberries. I loved the cherries, and how grown-up I felt! I had a grey coat with pink trim around the button holes. How I loved that coat, continuing to wear it even when it became too short in the arms and length.

Prom dresses were never a favorite of mine, as I am more a tailored person than a fancy party dress person, and I was glad when that era was behind me. There were the pleated wool skirts, matching sweaters, and coordinated handbags and shoes of my days in college. Matching outfits hung on two-part hangers and were arranged by color. A summer job at an affluent women's dress store in my hometown gave me the opportunity to acquire a marvelous wardrobe at cost, which I did, returning most of my salary to the store to purchase the merchandise. The green knit sheath dress, cinched at the waist with matching knit scarf and coordinated green and blue beaded necklace and earrings, were a favorite together with another Easter special. This time I was 20, wearing a grey fitted sheath, black patent belt, long sleeves with touch of ruffle at the wrist. It helped to have the slim body that showed off these clothes to advantage.

 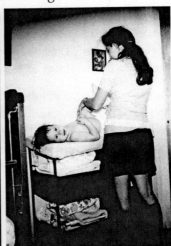

Joan posing at a museum   *Joan in a mini-skirt*

A few years later, married and a mother, I sported mini-skirts, high boots, and my proudly handmade macramé belts. Then I remember spending a weekend with friends and our respective young children and feeling so stylish in my brown velvet wide bell bottoms with matching tunic.

Then off to live in France for five years. I learned that no French woman ever goes to the grocery store without being perfectly groomed and wearing a scarf. My husband gave me designer scarves as gifts and thus started my love of scarves. I remember the trip to Amsterdam and looking smart in slim blue culottes, Irish sweater, matching hat, and high boots; the orange-flowered outfit I couldn't resist buying on Rue du Fauborg Saint-Honoré; and visiting the President of IBM France in my New Year's Yves St. Laurent grey straight skirt and azure blouse.

Clothes became more casual: running shorts, sweats, tennis outfits, jeans. But anything can be dressed up with a scarf.

(April 2, 2009)

People in My Life

People in my life whom I have lost touch with but still carry in my heart:

1. In Bayonne, New Jersey, elementary school, Our Lady Star of the Sea, Patricia McFadden was in my class. Wry and thin, pale skin, freckles, blond hair, blue eyes, not a beauty but an interesting and arresting face. She was always talking, getting into mischief and into trouble with the nuns, except for one daring deed. Ignoring all protocol, she dyed her hair green for St. Patrick's Day. Since the school was located in the Irish section of town, not only was she forgiven, but I even thought I saw a twinkle in those nun's eyes.

2. In Holy Family Academy, a Catholic high school for girls in Bayonne, Judy Padgorski and I battled it out for number one in class. I never felt any animosity towards me from Judy, and my feelings toward her were competitive but neutral. She was naturally bright but did nothing but study; she participated in no activities. Perhaps she was self-conscious as she was not attractive; can you call someone ugly when there is inner beauty? She was very tall, thin, angular, with small eyes set close together, a long sharp nose and angular chin. I was fascinated by the mechanisms of her face when she spoke. I wonder if she has gone on to achieve greatness and is happy.

3. Notre Dame College, Staten Island, New York. I commuted to college and rode every day with Evelyn Finnegan, from Bayonne, over the Bayonne Bridge to Staten Island and back again in the evening, and I contributed to the gas and the tolls. It wasn't a close friendship, more one of convenience, but she was always very supportive of me. At the freshman assembly when we were asked if anyone would like to share their talent, she stood up and said, "Joan Meehan can sing," and launched me in my singing career at college. I was a good listener to her in the endless stories about her uncle, the Bishop, how important he was and how he took her to many events with him. Is she alone and well, married or widowed? I don't know.

4. Graduate School, Rutgers Institute of Microbiology, New Brunswick, New Jersey. I was a Ph.D. student in microbiology and Dr. Carl Schaffner was my advisor. He was a brilliant man but, not trusting women, he had never taken one as a student. For some reason he made an exception for me, and I vowed not to let him down. The first cloud of suspicion crossed his face when I announced in my second year that I was going to get married. I know he believed that this should not be part of the plan. However, being the charming and gracious man that he was, he volunteered to provide all the flowers for the wedding. The flowers were orchids, which he grew in greenhouses on his property in a profusion of colors. All I had to tell him were the bridesmaids' colors and he said done. There was white for me and lavender and turquoise for the wedding party and beautiful pastel colors for the church. I was so indebted to him. All he asked in return was that I continue diligently with my research, which was actually his research, help him publish, and finish my degree. I promised in my heart that I would do that as that is what I wanted as well.

Fate determined a different path and shortly after my marriage I became pregnant, and ten months after the wedding had my first child. In his eyes I could have changed my name to Judas. He didn't rant or rave or even say anything but I felt the disbelief and disappointment in his body language. I drove the final nail into his heart when I announced that I would not finish the doctorate but write a master's thesis and leave. I wrote a good thesis, describing the structure of the antibiotic Gentamicin, which we produced in the lab, isolated, and identified. It was a promise of what more I could have been.

I heard that he never, ever accepted a female graduate student, not good for future women scientists. For all the good he did for me, for his trust and vulnerability, I hold him in my heart.

(April 20, 2009)

Joan posing in front of orchids at a flower show in New York City, 1965

Why Do I Make Time for Creative Expression?

Throughout my life, I have utilized some type of creative expression. In graduate school, I readily accepted my artist neighbor, June Safford's, suggestion that I paint in the evening. It was a wonderful balance to a day spent in the microbiology lab analyzing, distilling, discussing, writing, and researching with my scientific colleagues. It absorbed my focus and energy and gave me great pleasure. From a practical viewpoint, being poor graduate students, we could not afford to buy artwork to adorn the walls of our apartment. We then showcased my paintings, with Michael framing them once completed.

My painting continued when I moved to Katonah, New York, and met and painted with Ann Dolorian. Again, living in Paris in the 1970's, I painted with Bert DuAime and Kathy McCormick and did live-model drawings in Marie Cohen's Paris apartment. Living in Neuilly in 1982-1985, I did pastels led by a wonderful artist. We met at the Marymount School. Back in the US in 1985, living in New Canaan, I was fortunate to have the Silvermine Guild Art Center close by and attended the model drawing sessions and a watercolor class. However, I also started a paralegal certification program at Manhattanville College in Purchase, New York, and stopped the art classes to devote what free time I had after taking care of my family to studying for the certification. Now, I have the opportunity to paint in watercolor with Georgia Young, who comes to my house. I am so grateful to her.

My other creative pursuits have been studying photography and developing my own prints while living in Wilton, Connecticut, and creative French cooking including lessons while living in Neuilly and extensive meal preparation for guests while living in France and also back in the US after each stay in Paris. The creative cooking lasted from being a newlywed until I went to law school in 1992, at which time I asked Michael if he would take over the responsibility for food shopping and cooking dinner, and he agreed.

(July 7, 2009)

Chapter 3 –
"Paint a Watercolor for a Child": Joan's Poetry

Gratitude

The friends in our writing group
We open our hearts, write, and share
I look for poetry and love to read it now
It gives my life new meaning

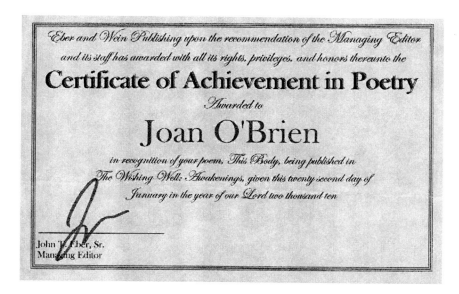

This Body

This body housed a ballet dancer,
a tap dancer, a ballroom dancer.
This body wore two-pieced bathing suits
and a Speedo one piece for swimming laps.

This body had slim legs that looked great in high heels,
and a waist with no rolls around or below it.
This body loved yoga and did it well,
with flat stomach and athletic arms.

An intruder, lymphedema, invaded this body,
slowly over the years, left arm, right arm,
right leg, left leg, feet, toes, pelvic area.
Does my body feel as sad as I am?

This body, my shelter, my refuge
for so many years
has changed forever
Can I accept this?
I have to; there is no choice.

Stride forward, you know what to do.
Help this body as much as you can
Be kind, be gentle, be thankful
for all the years of beauty.

*(January 5, 2009; published February 3, 2010 in The Wishing Well:
Awakenings, ed. John T. Eber, Sr. Eber & Wein, 2009.)*

Flat

I was an adolescent full of promise
I was a young woman in love
Then a wife, a mother
I breastfed four children
I lived in France
I had dreams of a career
I went to law school at 50

Then cancer hit
May 1, 1995—last day of classes
Lumpectomy, graduation, chemotherapy, mastectomy, radiation

I survived
I thrived

Lymphedema—wrapping and massage
Recurrence in lymph node 2003—chemotherapy
Then cancer hit other breast
September 16, 2004—mastectomy, chemotherapy, radiation
Implants give girlish form—all is well
Recurrence in skin—chemotherapy
   and again
Cellulitis infection
   and again
Implant infected
Both sides removed

More than flat—concave
Now a Crone
A wife, a mother, a grandmother
Wisdom, love, and compassion to share
Hope to impart
Survive and thrive

(April 29, 2007)

Mother's Day 2007

I have no breasts
I have no hair

I have swelling in my arms and leg
I have breast cancer in the skin of my chest

I have a husband
I have four children and three grandchildren

I have faith
I have hope in healing my disease

I am here today
Happy Mother's Day to me

(May 13, 2007)

Now I'm 65

Sixty-five on 6/5
A memorable birthday for many reasons

I am celebrating being 65 on 6/5
My husband and children are here to celebrate with me
Alyssa from California
JP from Colorado via California
Chris, Aidan, and Lisa from Colorado
Will and Sarah from Boston via Princeton

Three days ago my husband arranged a surprise party
Family and friends from all walks of life

The ones you love are life's most precious gifts

(June 5, 2007)

Julia

You have to be strong and have hope
You have to build up your body to withstand
    whatever treatment may shrink your tumor
You have to trust that the doctors will know
    the right treatment to prescribe
You have to hold on, Julia.

(June 14, 2008; for Julia Arliss who passed away on June 20, 2008)

A Prayer for Guidance

I am nervous
I am scared
But I know I am doing the right thing
Help me Lord I pray
Give me this chance to breathe easier and cope
Give me more time with my loved ones
That I may be grateful for another day of beauty

(June 3, 2009)

Gratitude [1]

For this day
Wintry and cold
Crystalline white snow cover on the grass

The parking lot at Bennett was full
But the valet was waiting to assist
I gratefully gave him the keys to my car
On this cold wintry day

The friends in our writing group
We open our hearts, write, and share
I look for poetry and love to read it now
It gives my life new meaning
I go to the edge

There is always more to discover
Love to feel
Bonds to make and strengthen like
The vine circling the tree
Guard this feeling
This flutter in the heart and gut
This excitement for life as it now is
In me and around me
The fertile field of gratitude

(December 8, 2008)

Conversation with my Body

Breathe in deeply and breathe out, very deep breathing
This feels so good to my body
This I can do, several times a day
It calms and relaxes me
It stimulates the deep lymph nodes
Moves that lymph fluid along

In my dreams I'm a wisp of a thing
My spirit is bright and breezy in my body
It loves fields of flowers and butterflies
It runs and skips full of love and life
Happy, carefree, and flowing

In reality, I lumber more
Work hard at staying agile and limber
Heavier limbs and thicker waist
Aches and pains that come and go, come and go
Dear body, you need some love, some caring
You need to be nurtured and encouraged
I will do this for you, dear friend

I promise rest and good nutrition
Maybe some wine now and then
I know you like that
Will you work with me to make you stronger?
Can mind, spirit, and heart collaborate with
Bones, muscles, and tendons?
To accept discipline of exercise, walking,
Tai Chi, and yoga
Let's do it, dear body,
It is our way to a comfortable life together

(January 12, 2009)

Rituals

Some rituals I have had to give up because of medical issues:
    My manicures and pedicures
    My deep, hot soaking bubble baths
    Deep-tissue, full-body massage
These were some of the rituals I loved—now part of fond memories.

There are actions I want to become rituals:
    Meditation and deep yogic breathing
    Yoga and Tai Chi exercises to move the energy
        upon waking in the morning
    Daily sit-ups and stretches to keep the body toned
They are a part of my "to-do" and "to-be-ritualized" list.
    Is tomorrow the day I will start?

Some habits happen without thinking:
    Washing my face and brushing my teeth every night
    Making the bed first thing in the morning
    Opening and closing certain blinds every day
    Putting my purse on the same chair
    Charging my phone every night
    Calling my children often, nearly every day
    Kissing my husband goodbye as he leaves for work
    Taking the time to marvel at the mystery of a sunset
        and at the beauty and delicateness of a flower

More and more . . .
    The simple mindfulness of the sunset and a flower
    The voice of a family member or a friend
    The gathering of community at mass,
        at yoga or Tai Chi, and at writing
. . . have become the rituals that sustain me,
        that wrap the golden thread around me,
        that hold me together when fragile
        and nourish my body and soul.

(November 24, 2008)

Tai Chi in Two Movements

Prose Poem

Take a long breath in and let a long breath out. Stand tall, relaxed, tail bone tucked under, knees flexed. Arms are light and delicate but strong. As you move, feel the energy the Chinese call "Chi." It compresses and expands as you move your hands together and apart, as you twist from the waist, from your center.

Finally, after more than a year, I have learned the movements of the short form of Tai Chi we practice in class. Now that the movements have become automatic, I can concentrate on the breath, long and even, and my body's movements, smooth and flowing. Now I feel the energy of my body in the universe.

Poem

Take a long breath in
Let a long breath out
Stand tall, relaxed
Tail bone tucked under, knees flexed
Arms are light and delicate but strong
Move and feel the energy called Chi
Feel it compress and expand
As you move your hands together and apart
As you twist from the waist
From your center
As I learn the movements of a form of Tai Chi
The movements become automatic
I can concentrate on the breath, long and even
And on my body's movements, smooth and flowing
Now I feel the energy of my body in the universe

(June 19, 2008)

Loving Acceptance

I want to be limber and flexible as I age. I want to be graceful and delicate as a flower on a substantial stem, swaying in the breeze, lifting its face to the sun in salutation.

I have found this goal possible to achieve through my practice of yoga. Over the years, I have learned to be in the moment and listen as my body instructs me on what it can do on a particular day in class.

Yoga teaches us "do no harm"—do nothing in practice that would cause pain or injury. I have found that my forward bend does not extend as far as before, and that Headstands and Shoulder Stands are no longer a part of my repertoire. There are so many other positions, however—twists and stretches—that make my body say, "Aah, yes, this is good." But, oh, there is that twinge in the back again, and I know what problems it can cause. So I ease back, shift, and modify.

I am not in competition with anyone in class. I only need to account for myself, and I have given myself loving acceptance.

(June 19, 2008; formerly entitled "Yoga for an Aging Yogini"
and published in Fit Yoga, October 2008)

Reflection on the Write Retreat

Happily I participated
Grateful to be there among Stanford alumni
Learning and sharing together
Appreciating so much in common

There was snack time with coffee and cookies
After the break, back to work, back to the workshop
Until lunchtime
Lunch outside on the deck with interesting people
A glass of white wine to accent a delicious meal

Saturday, a memorable day
A day climaxed with a ride down the mountain
In the middle of the night
Seeking lower elevation
Easing difficult breathing

Returning to Will and Sarah's house
Celebrating Mother's Day all together
Knowing of the surprise coming starting Thursday
For my dear Alyssa
Draping her in love from family and friends
For her 40th birthday

(July 17, 2009)

Routine

A long deep sleep last night
No need for Vicodin
Tylenol at 5 am for comfort
Then hard to get up

Crazy dream last night
A mergers-and-acquisitions yoga Kabbalah
Ken Griesser and family also had access
Someone else too I could not remember
Only I logged on
And spoke quietly to myself

Oxygen tube was partly out of my nose
Then this morning I realized it had been shut off
And lights put on
Efforts to wake me up

Up at the table
Foot soaking in cold water
The same routine starts again
When will people tire of taking care of me this way
I wonder
When will they stop visiting, bringing meals
Will I get better, or linger on the same, or worse

Time to dust away these thoughts like unwanted cobwebs
Finish the John Tinker project
Read a few pages of the many books stacked up waiting
Paint a beautiful watercolor
Review Father Ian's papers and prayer
Share this beautiful new day with Alyssa and Michael

(June 6, 2009)

Dance of Distress

Words burned into my stomach with great pain
Another Ativan, I begged
Hot water bottle
Bucket on my bed just in case
Finally I had to get out of bed and use the bathroom
The Ativan kicked in

I fell back asleep, back to dream land
There was dancing, generating energy, going to a restaurant
And discussions with a doctor as today I had to feel
Someone else's pain
I was hopeful I could avoid this

In the morning light I realized it was me
Whatever may have caused it
And the hot water bottle and Ativan helped

It still aches this morning
Some tea, some toast, meds and now upstairs
For sponge bath and a new day

It will be a beautiful day

(June 7, 2009)

A New Day

Birds sang after dark
I was trying to finish the John Tinker project
Almost done
Sitting in chair, leg wrapped, Miltex and ear done
Feeling peaceful

Oxygen tube in my hand instead of my nose
Apologized to Michael and Alyssa for uncooperativeness
They only think of my own good and needs
Remember that

Hope for sweet dreams and peaceful sleep tonight
Tomorrow dawns a new day full of promise
A day to mold like clay in our hands
What will transpire, who will we see, what will we feel?

We are happy and positive
Goodnight

(June 7, 2009)

"I will meditate on love tonight, on loving myself unconditionally as well as giving and receiving love unconditionally from others. I pray that this realization will be my healing, my lifting up from any darkness or despair."

Needing Help

Up at 5:30 am
Enough sleep
No stomach pain during the night
Hot in bed, ready to get out
Heavy breathing, good to sit up
Begin another day

Some writing, some relaxing, some visiting
Perhaps see Anne at Dr. Hall's office for some relief

Had breakfast early—ready for sponge bath
Let's do something different today
Chores, Tai Chi, read, watch wedding video

Finish up loose ends—John Tinker Project, Not Giving Up,
Going through writings
Be positive and happy on this new day

This is the day the Lord has made
Let us rejoice and be glad
I feel a need to reflect some more on Father Ian's work
I look at the orchids, purple, majestic, still,
They haven't changed overnight
I haven't changed either

Must relieve labored breathing
It's one thing that I can do to help me

Help me Lord, help me anyone

(June 8, 2009)

Next Steps

Each day is a new day
A day of opportunity
A next step, a baby step
Into the future

What birds will appear
More cardinals and blue jays
Will a hummingbird make a most wanted appearance
Will I look at colors and shapes
With an artist's eye
Will I see the structure of flowers
As well as the values
Analyze the details of a leaf
A blade of grass

Will my mind fly to a high branch of a tree
Look at the depths of the sky
At the panorama below me
The beauty of nature, God's creation

Will the wind lift me gently
As on a magic carpet
Take me over rolling fields
Meadows of wild flowers
Lush valleys and snow-capped mountains
Deserts and oceans

Will God hold me closer every day
Give me strength and grace
All my heart continue to fill with faith, hope, and love
And shine open for all to see
Will Michael be happy
And continue his loving care
He gives so freely and tenderly
What can I do
Oh what can I do
In each next step

(July 26, 2009)

Savor Each Moment

Night is here
Nearly time for welcome sleep
A little early tonight
Skyped with Alyssa and JP, Ariana, and Liam
Nice way to end the evening

Busy day
Lunch, radiation, back home for hot fudge sundae
Time for rest then Minerva with physical therapy
Msgr. Scheyd with communion
Vivian Howell with Reiki

Feeling tired from radiation
Found another lymph node at base of skull
Weight is going up slightly
Draining is going well
Michael and I are humming along smoothly

Jen, Ariana, and Liam are coming out
July 25 for an overnight
Then Alyssa will come
I look forward to all that

Enjoy each day
Savor each moment
Rest and heal with sleep
Tomorrow dawns a new day, a busy day
Another gift from God for me

(July 16, 2009)

Being Normal

Listening to music
Friends bringing and staying for dinner
It seems so normal

There is an ache in the catheter area
Some dried blood
Is there a problem?

Its operation facilitates my normal
Draining twice a day
Enabling me to breathe

Radiation continues, five more days
Do your work
Make my ear normal

I yearn for more mobility
To practice gentle yoga and Tai Chi
To walk with more stability or unaided

To lift my legs into the car
To move into the car without losing my breath
To smile more with ease

To blossom like a flower
Always accepting what I am now
That is my normal

(June 19, 2009)

Fresh Start

I look forward to each moment
Embrace what may fall in my path
Pick up a burden and shoulder it
Embrace a joy and hold it to my heart
Not giving up
Going on each day
Baby step by baby step
Covering the terrain of my life
This is the now for me
To accept and actualize
And live each moment

(July 3, 2009)

Michael and Joan visiting Giverny, France in 2005

Long-lasting

I love the white lilies that continue to bloom and last
A symbol of strength, life, and hope
I identify with those white lilies
Giving me endurance

I will continue to thrive as best as I can
For myself, my husband, and my children
I pray for patience and compassion to others
I thank God for my blessings

I feel free and happy as the little birds
Numerous outside in my yard
Flying from tree to bush to flowers
Chirping and singing gaily

Sunshine kissing the patio this afternoon
Everyone sitting together outside
Long-lasting happiness

(July 4, 2009)

Imagining God

What do we imagine God to be?
A white light
A perfect spirit
We take on faith what we deduce
We won't know until the time arrives

(June 16, 2009)

My Time

When my time comes
Let it come beautifully and peacefully
Let me be surrounded by my loved ones
My husband, my children
Holding my hands
All there together
Telling me I am loved

I know this
But want to hear the words
Looking into my eyes
So I can show them my such deep love
For each one of them

I will miss growing older with them
Seeing my grandchildren grow up
How fortunate was grandmother
Living to 97
Seeing so many of her grandchildren
Graduate
Marry
And have their own children
Even when she could no longer see
She embraced them with her other senses

I've done so well on this cancer journey
I sometimes wonder why I hit this snag
Did not receive a cure
I did change as a person
I became a better person
I would not give that up

Walk with me gently through the day and night
Grant me sweet dreams and healing sleep
Until the dawn of a new day

(June 19, 2009)

Ready

Ready to die—not yet
    Ready to be more mobile—yes
    Ready for another peaceful sleep
    Ready to paint another watercolor
    Ready to see my writing group

I am ready for my daily and weekly rituals.
I am ready for another night of peaceful sleep, essence of flowers on the
    bottom of my feet to the extent of space left over after wrapping.
I am ready to paint another watercolor next week.
I am ready to see my Healing through Writing group and write with
    them at my house.
I am ready to be more mobile if I can, by stretching and exercising.
I am ready to be drained every morning and evening to help me
    breathe easier.
I am ready to spend time with friends, talk on the phone in limited
    time bits.
I am ready to keep taking my chemotherapy, do my wrapping, and do
    what I can to make each day a special day.
And I am more than ready to spend time with my children and my
    husband, feeling our love for each other.

But I am not ready to die—not yet.
It may be that I have not given up, have not waved the white flag of
    surrender.
I don't feel so miserable that I can't take another day.
There are still words to be written, memories and feelings to share.
I actually feel better most of the time—
Even the rain does not dampen my spirit as long as I can be warm
    enough and breathe.
I realize that I am not afraid to die. I am just not ready yet.
I am not looking for years down the road as that could be hard in my
    present condition.
I can acclimate to living as I am by surrounding myself with laughter
    and beauty, faith, hope, and love.

I am preparing for death, spiritually and mentally, and live each day.

There are no forecasts, no deadlines, even the famous to-do list is not as common, as before it was my every day companion.

This is the day the Lord has made. Let us give thanks and be glad.

(June 20, 2009)

What I Want

I want to live each day with laughter and fun
I want to look nice and feel good every day without trying too hard
Most of all, I want to be mindful, mindful, mindful
So that I don't zone out when someone is talking

So that I don't pull into the garage too sharply and knock over the paint cans stacked in the corner and catch the handle of a gallon of white paint on my bumper, causing its pure whiteness to spread ever so slowly on the cement garage floor

So that I don't spend the next hour soaking up the paint with newspapers, then mopping it up with rags, then calling my husband to give him a heads-up before he comes home and sees the vandalism for himself

I want to see life like a child
I want to love and embrace the world every day
I want to dance in the rain
I want to walk barefoot in dewy grass
I want to ride a bike with my grandchildren
I want them to confide in me
I want not to miss my own children so much

I want to let go and let live
I want to be a good person, friend, wife, mother, lover
I want to live a long time

(September 18, 2008)

Planting Seeds of Hope

As time goes on
Planting seeds of hope becomes harder
Physically and mentally
The physical obstruction of bending to the earth
Because of swelling
The mental obstruction of reality, of knowing
Your body is not bouncing back as it should

Look at it a different way
What can I pass on to my family
Someday—whenever that may be—none of us knows when
Words lovingly spoken but also recorded on a page
A flower in watercolor painted to the best
Of my ability and given to a child
A smile and touch to my caregiver husband
For my appreciation for all he does for me

Acknowledgement of the care and concern of my sons
Rejoicing in the love and nurturing of my daughter
Two women who love each other so deeply it almost hurts
Nourishing the hope to leave a legacy of beauty and love
Nourishing the hope to have a long time
Yet to accomplish these goals
Not giving up no matter what happens
Keeping the fire of hope and adventure within me
Accepting whatever may come with grace and dignity

(June 10, 2009)

CHAPTER 4 –
"IN THE PRESENCE OF FAMILY": CELEBRATION OF LOVED ONES

My family, my children are long-lasting. To me, they are everlasting because they will continue to carry me in their hearts and memory.

(July 4, 2009)

I know it will be hard to say goodbye but I believe there will be grace in the next life and that my memory will carry on and continue in my children and grandchildren.

(September 2, 2009)

[Writing] expresses me, who I am, so that my children and grandchildren will glimpse my heart and soul.

(July 7, 2009)

O'Brien family with nephew Hans Griesser's family in Lake Tahoe, 2006

In the Presence of Family

I have a wonderful, wonderful family.

I'm sure that my appreciation of family was nurtured as a child. I was
an only child. I remember from the earliest years how I yearned for a
brother or sister. I know my mother, especially, shared these feelings.
But it did not happen. Over the years, my mother and I grew closer
and closer in our own relationship, one not only of mother and
daughter, but also of girlfriend and girlfriend. I saw much less of my
father as he worked at two jobs, evening hours at his regular
employment with Sun Oil Company and weekends and some hours
during the day at a second job to bring in extra income.

My mother, Joan Meehan, was Ukrainian, and my father, Martin
Meehan, was Irish. Each had their own parish church. As a young
child and teenager I often went to the Ukrainian Catholic Church with
my mother. I loved the Ukrainian choir with its unique chanting, the
church rich in icons, candles and liturgies, and the Ukrainian
community.

My father attended the Irish church, Our Lady Star of the Sea, and I
also attended mass there on some Sundays and went to St. Mary's

Catholic School, associated with this parish church. After elementary school, I attended an all girls' Catholic high school, Holy Family Academy, and upon graduation received a full tuition scholarship to an all women's catholic college, the College of Notre Dame, on Staten Island, New York. I lived at home and commuted to school every day. I loved Notre Dame and was active in debate, singing groups including the baroque ensemble, and did very well academically.

In March of my sophomore year, when I was 19, my mother died unexpectedly of a ventricular fibrillation in her heart. I was devastated and had trouble breathing for about a year. Since my father worked nights, I stayed with a friend and her parents for several months. I also had another close friend from college and was often at her home for dinner.

I graduated from college with a Bachelor of Science degree in chemistry and started graduate school at Rutgers University in New Brunswick, New Jersey, going for a Ph.D. in chemistry. Through a friend, I obtained a summer position right after graduation from college working at the Institute of Microbiology in the chemistry of microbial products department. I spent the first year in the chemistry department and found it very hard, although I enjoyed my teaching assistantship to freshmen at Rutgers College. I had commuted to the Institute of Microbiology all summer, nearly five hours round trip, and in the fall I decided to live at the university in the graduate dormitory called Stonier Hall.

I met Michael O'Brien in October 1964, in the graduate lounge at Stonier Hall. He was studying for a Ph.D. in computer science. He was also telling jokes and playing cards, and I thought how frivolous as I was busy marking my chemistry papers with my classroom colleague, John Rose. Michael came over and John introduced us, and Michael started chatting. I made up some answers, such as I had six siblings and so on, as I was not trying to impress. He asked if I would have coffee with him the next day, and I agreed. At coffee, he asked if I would go to the movies with him the next day. I believe it was the weekend. I do not remember the movie, but I do remember that afterwards we went to Washington Rock, a steep drive up to a rock monument overlooking the twinkling lights below. It was where Washington viewed his troops. When we were there, he asked me to marry him. I was flabbergasted and said we had to talk about it later, as I was already seriously dating someone else. We stayed up and talked all night in the broom closet.

He was pinned to a young woman and severed that relationship the next day. Finally, I resisted no longer. He had completely won my heart, and I knew he was the one for me. I broke off my relationship with my boyfriend, causing no end of conflict. Both of them sent me flowers and little gifts often, and I was very upset, although the girls in my dorm thought it was so romantic. My ex-boyfriend made a surprise visit to my dorm on my birthday. I don't know how he was able to gain entrance to my room, perhaps by my roommate, but I opened the door and there he was. It was very embarrassing. I did not want to discuss anything. The rest is history.

We were engaged in 1965 and married in August 1966. Chris was born ten months after our wedding. So our own family began. We were so much in love and still are.

I made up for being an only child by gaining Michael's eight siblings and his lovely parents, Beatrice and Maurice O'Brien. Although I no longer saw my mother's siblings nor her extended family after her death, it no longer concerned me. I just would have liked to know more about them and therefore my history.

I became pregnant with Alyssa, and she was born on May 17, 1969, nearly two years after Chris. During my pregnancy, my father became ill. We brought him to New Brunswick, where we were living in student housing. He was diagnosed with Hodgkin's disease, was treated at a hospital near us and went into remission. After staying with us again for a short while, he returned to his flat in Bayonne in his sister's house for several months. Unbeknownst to me, she told him that in order to stay there he had to turn over my inheritance, including his stock certificates, to her name, which he did. During that time, he met a woman, gave her a ring, and became engaged.

We all thought he would be fine, but the cancer returned, and he was brought to us right after Alyssa was born. He again received chemotherapy, but he died two months later on July 20, 1969, the day Neil Armstrong walked on the moon. We took care of the funeral arrangements, and it was at that time that his employer told me about the stock certificates. I felt betrayed, but there was nothing I could do about it. In addition, I had my own wonderful family which meant the world to me. I did not need his siblings nor his extended family in my life. I carried on very happily without my father's family, and they never reached out to me.

We moved from Rutgers' student housing to our own house, our first purchase, in Fanwood, New Jersey, in 1969. It was a lovely house for us. A green cape with awnings and shutters, a manicured flower bedding, a spacious yard, three bedrooms, kitchen, bathroom, living room, and a windowed enclosed porch. We lived there for over a year and made wonderful friends, the Beinsteins and Goldfingers. We had good social adventures with them, saw them often, and our children became good friends with theirs.

Michael was transferred to White Plains, New York, and we sold our Fanwood house and bought a brand new home in Katonah, New York. I loved my new home and all the newness of it. The one big disappointment was that shortly after we moved, after a heavy rain, and despite having a sump pump, the basement flooded with over six inches of water, and many items were ruined or destroyed. I remember the fire department coming to pump out the water, and Chris and Alyssa, at four and two years old, being very excited.

It was also in Katonah that I started oil paintings of local scenes, painting with an artist friend Ann Dolorian. I was also heavily involved as a volunteer at the Katonah library, which had an excellent art collection. You could borrow a painting to hang in your home for a period of one month.

I also started taking piano lessons with a young man who came to the house every Friday for an hour lesson. Chris and Alyssa cooperated very well by either playing quietly or listening. I also found out I was pregnant with Jean-Paul. So it was not very appealing when Michael told me that IBM wanted to send him to Paris, and he wanted to go. He said it would only be for two years, so I agreed. And the best part is that it turned out to be a wonderful five years.

(August 14, 2009)

The Proposal

I met my husband one month after I entered graduate school. We lived in a co-ed dorm, and I was in the basement lounge with other grad students, diligently marking my students' chemistry test papers, specifically lab papers from graduate analysis. As a new college graduate, now a teaching assistant in chemistry, I had to work hard and be serious to exert some authority in my all male freshman class. I looked about the same age as them. Rutgers was an all men's college at that time, so I was absolutely not a student. I always dressed nicely in stark contrast to the student attire of clothes barely held together: ragged shorts, shirts with holes, and loafers coming apart at the toes. The little love notes which were slipped between calculations and formulas were charming, but they didn't turn my head.

Then, one night as I was steadfastly working, a good looking Irish lad, Michael O'Brien, entered the room and proceeded to play bridge and tell jokes. Humph, I thought. He just wants to have fun; he should be studying. Then, there he was standing in front of me, introducing himself. I wasn't flustered. I had a steady, serious, no-nonsense boyfriend back home. So I played along in a light manner and even made up some things which felt liberating to me. He said he was one of nine; I said I was one of six, instead of the truth of being an only child.

"Let's meet for coffee tomorrow," he said.

"Fine," I said. The next day, the coffee was good, the conversation stimulating, and he was good looking.

"Will you go to the movies with me tomorrow?" Tomorrow was Saturday, so I said fine.

We went to the movies; I don't recall the movie. I just remember the historical tour afterwards. He was from the area and drove me up a long, winding steep road to the top of a mountain and a place called Washington Rock. It is where Washington viewed his troops below. We saw the city lights twinkling below and the starry sky, but the ominous bulk of the rock and the darkness made me shiver. He gave me his coat and said, "You are the woman I want to marry." That was my proposal after two days, followed by many hours of earnest discussion, including that I had a boyfriend back home. Both men courted me every day with flowers delivered to my room and little presents appearing in my mailbox.

Everyone in the dorm felt I was so lucky, but I was miserable. I had to make a decision. After six or seven months, Michael O'Brien won the contest.

One day he said he had to go to New York for the day; he didn't say why. When he came back, he asked me to come to his dorm room, and he made us some tea on the little hot plate he had. He was so nervous, he spilt some of the tea on my ear! His bed had been pushed into the groove in the wall, which made it a couch. The tea was on a ledge behind me. He started to put his arm around me and hit the tea cup. I realize now that this was the beginning of 42 years of comedy sequences. I still had no clue of what was going on or perhaps I wanted to be clueless.

Then out of the pocket of his brown tweed jacket, he pulled out a little black box. Oh my gosh, I thought, this is it. Am I too young at 23? There wasn't time for protest. He opened the box and there was a perfect Tiffany-style diamond. He did not go down on his knee. He just took the ring out of the box and slipped it on my finger.

(January 8, 2009)

Michael and Joan on their honeymoon in the Bahamas, 1966

My Husband

We have been married for 42 ½ years. We grew up together and are growing old together. In our minds, our bodies are still young, although the mark of time is evident to the eye. He is my best friend, even if stubborn and controlling sometimes. He is my only lover. We have been through so many experiences together: his long business career and now teaching career, law school for me at age 50, the challenge of raising four children with all the emotion entailed in that endeavor, the apprehension and support of me in my thirteen-year journey with breast cancer. It is what it is. This is my life. This is his life. Breathe deeply. Accept and be grateful.

(December 4, 2008)

My Caregiver

A strong awareness of the term caregiver came to me when I made the Pilgrimage to Lourdes this past May, with my husband as my caregiver. There were separate sessions for caregivers in Lourdes so that the caregiver could discuss issues common among themselves. One key issue was the frustration of the caregiver that the person they were taking care of wasn't listening to them or became angry when told what he or she should do. That in turn made the caregiver angry. When I discussed this with my husband, I told him that the ill person doesn't like to be told what to do even though they are being told for their own good. They want to keep whatever control over their lives that they can hold. Out of that discussion came my understanding that it had to be difficult for my husband as caregiver. He goes food shopping and cooks dinner. He wraps my lymphedema limbs every day. He worries and cares for me. He, like many men, wants to fix whatever is wrong. He has certain and definite ideas. I, on the other hand, although practical, am more of a dreamer and sentimentalist. My emotions and heart may rule over my head and common sense. In this manner, I frustrate him. I appear unthankful.

I want him to know that I love him and am deeply thankful for everything he does for me. The gift of awareness of his specialness may have been a little miracle of Lourdes. I am very grateful for my husband who is my caregiver and so much more.

(December 8, 2008)

Michael and Joan on a pilgrimage to Lourdes, 2008

Memory of Father's Day

I am with two Dads today, Michael and Chris: Michael a veteran and Chris a relatively new Dad with many experiences and adventures ahead of him with his son, Aidan.

Each child is different, a different personality, which we try to guide with our values while allowing them to express themselves, although not anticipating the Indian war paint before the plane ride, nor the orange sink in the classroom at the American School of Paris, nor the liverwurst on Mr. Beswitch's projector. We, Michael and I, dealt with these actions in our own way. Being the goody-two-shoes, I was bewildered at this action by my flesh and blood; Michael, not so subject to society's constraints, just laughed.

That is how we were good for each other, a balance of one another. Now I have changed tremendously, and he has also. We have mellowed together. It has been 43 years of marriage (in August), and 42 father's days.

We had different ways of coping, different styles, but we loved our children with a passion as we do now. The hardest thing in our early years was communication. The difference between men and women was so evident then. When there was a problem, he became quiet and kept it all inside. He did not want to talk about it unless he was completely at the end of his patience, and then he would blurt out some hard statement which shocked me because I wasn't part of the thought process that led to the words.

I begged that he talk to me and discuss. I interpreted his non-answer that he was angry with me, and I would say what is wrong, and he would say nothing. IBM work stress did this to him many times. It took me years to realize that he was not angry with me.

Now I look back with a different lens. I only see his love and kindness and boundless generosity. I know that I could not have asked for a better husband or father. He cares for me now, his wife, but I am as dependent as a child. I feel so blessed this Father's Day to celebrate with my husband and son. I love them so very much.

(June 21, 2009)

Laughter of the O'Brien Men

The ripple of Will's laugh lightens the air. Chris's jokes come almost out of nowhere, with a serious face followed by a big smile. Michael always is ready with a joke. I have to say when. Aidan is following in the footsteps of these O'Brien men. And I am encouraged to say something witty if I can. Laughter is the best medicine. One of the talents of my many-talented family is the ease to laughter, not taking oneself too seriously. It is the balm that soothes the hurt, the frame for the smile; it is a release of a puff of happiness. We remember funny incidents for a long time, and yes, cherish them. There is a time for every season—a time to be serious and a time to laugh. I vote for much laughter, more and more laughter to carry me on a magic carpet to dream land.

(June 2, 2009)

O'Brien family portrait, 1991

Transformation

I spent time with my son, Chris
We sat and talked
It was a sharing of the soul and heart
Words spoken and memories relived
Love flowed unconditional and nonjudgmental

I spent time with my son, Chris
We walked Boulder Creek on a beautiful October day
The sun was warm, the breeze gentle, the brook babbled
Blue sky with puffy clouds, faint trace of the moon
So many lush plants and scents overwhelming the senses
Even a snake gliding across the path so beautiful
A tiny empty bird's nest perfect as a work of art
The time together a priceless gift

(October 3, 2008)

Chris's Birthday

Darkness at 7 am, but still the flowers on the patio give off a color.
Today is Chris's birthday; he is 42 years old. He seems happy. He has
and loves his son, Aidan. He and Lisa, Aidan's mother, have a good
relationship, and he and Erin are getting along well. He has a job
which brings in steady income and is working on his financial
problems. Most important, he is sober. I am so proud of him for that.

Another day reveals itself.

(June 9, 2009)

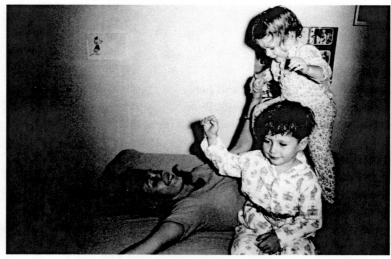

Joan with Chris and Alyssa, 1971

Joan with Aidan, 2002

Joan with Chris and Aidan, 2009

Joan with Chris, May 2009

Erin's Sessions

When I was in Colorado, I had an energy treatment from Erin Love called core synchronism. I lay on a heated massage table, very comfortable with pillows under my head and under my knees and covered with a blanket. Erin explained that the goal was to clear any energy blockages and facilitate the flow of energy and lymph fluid through the body. It would be fine if I fell asleep. Normally, I have no problem falling asleep anywhere, especially prone on a comfortable table.

But as she touched her fingers lightly to my head, I felt tingling and itching and imagined light—white sparks and blue streaks. How could I possibly fall asleep with all of this going on?

The amazing thing was that there was something bothering me, a trivial event. During the session I realized how heavily it was weighing down my heart. It was as if a rock replaced my heart. I worked internally to turn that rock into softness like a ball of pliable dough, and it happened. I felt warmth and peace, which carried over to a night of sound sleep and sweet dreams.

You would think that I was now in an enlightened place forever. When I had another session a few days later, both Erin and I thought that we would find energy flowing and immediate relaxation. But we both had to work as hard as before.

(October 24, 2008)

I Am Grateful

For going to mass with Michael, JP, Jen, Ariana, and Liam
For having breakfast with Michael, JP, Chris, and Aidan
For going for a 40 minute walk looking at the Flatirons
For being able to breathe without effort
For being mindful about taking time for legs up the wall
For enjoying a beautiful day
For being here in Boulder
For being alive
For grace, courage, and fortitude.

(December 14, 2008)

Lisa Turner, Joan, Sarah, Alyssa, Jennifer and Anne Griesser in Boulder, 2002

The Gift

My daughter's cottage in Half Moon Bay, California, is surrounded by flowers outside spilling inside, luscious blooms of white, yellow, and pink. Sitting outside in the garden behind the cottage, nestled within three walls framed by lemon trees and lush shrubbery, I gaze at the numerous calla lilies: tall, strong, and elegant. I recall my mother holding them as her wedding bouquet in a photo taken 72 years ago. Yellow daffodils and purple violets carpet the border of the garden, bougainvillea vines its way along the fence, large bushes of hydrangea are just opening up, the flowers still green and delicate, and roses highlight a spot of red here and there. Fuschia, which I only know of in hanging baskets, have grown to small tree size, their pink and purple bells wafting in the gentle breeze.

I saw my first hummingbird, skimming the highest tree just above the robins who were busy flying from tree to tree and making nests with much chatter. Their favorite abode was the berry tree and with great delight they dive-bombed my daughter-in-law's brand new red Prius, obviously parked too close to their beloved tree, lavishly splashing the car in shades of blue, purple, white, and black.

I leaned back and closed my eyes savoring the delicious warmth of the sun, the smell of the clean sea air, and the comfort of a clear blue sky.

The round wooden table, resting on inlaid tiles in the center of the garden, was being set for lunch, with French table cloth and napkins and flowers in the center, of course. Wine glasses appeared, a bottle of Tavel, and my son-in-law, Laird, carried out a platter containing quiche, artichoke tarte, and tarte provencale which he had just purchased in the market that morning. A crisp green salad and warm French bread completed the menu. We were definitely in Provence!

If my cup could run fuller, it did as I looked around the table I was sharing with those I love, my husband, Michael, my daughter and son-in-law, Alyssa and Laird, and my son and daughter-in-law, Will and Sarah. I know that it does not get better than this moment in time.

(February 27, 2009)

Sarah, Will, Joan, Michael, Alyssa and Laird in Half Moon Bay, 2008

Alyssa and Joan, 1978

Alyssa and Joan, 2006

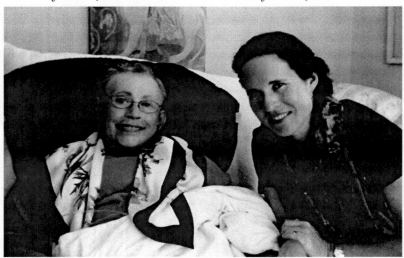

Joan and Alyssa, May 2009

Letter to Alyssa

I don't write letters usually. You are so incredible about sending me all those cards in addition to our speaking every day. This letter, then, is dedicated to you.

You are my love, my joy, as you have been since the time you were born. We did go through challenging teenage years. I beg your forgiveness for any ways that you have been hurt. I know we can't change the past, but I can't say things happen for the best or the way they should. I am so sorry.

My diagnosis was a turning point in us becoming closer and closer. I feel sometimes that we are one spirit, two hearts beating as one tied by ribbons of love. Your invitation to Tahoe honored me. Your encouragement to write gave me new direction, strength, and hope. Your being here has been one of the key ingredients in my coping and getting strength, my acceptance and adjustment.

I know you can't stay forever, and I know you will come back again. I know that you are Laird's wife, and the two of you need to be together—and I know you can't make a baby if you are not together. So that is my reason I can let you go, and the reason I have decided not to give in, to fight and keep going as long as I can. I am not trying to put pressure but just telling you how I feel.

I will miss so much writing with you and expressing my deepest feelings. I am looking forward to tomorrow as our golden day ahead of us, just as Sunday was. No one but us to do what we want: talk, write, walk, and share the space together.

I love you so, so much and I will miss you terribly, but I know I'll see you again before too long, as I have this summer of healing and working things out. It's all in the attitude, isn't it?

You are such an encouragement, saying, "Mom, you're doing great," during my tap, seeing me in the recovery room after the drain and always at home whatever I am doing. It empowers me. You empower me. I admire so much your intellect, your kindness, and your ability to teach so heartfully, to reach out to people so warmly and so unselfishly. I just love, love, love you. Mom.

(June 30, 2009)

The Decision

He was in his bedroom on the second floor. The large plate-glass window which opened outward as one piece was opened about ten inches. It was an opening through which an energetic, inquisitive, adorable four-year old boy could inadvertently lean too far and fall down—down to the French courtyard below.

As I walked into his bedroom, he turned his round face from the fascination of the view in front of him and his large brown eyes met mine. This child of beauty with the incredibly long dark brown eyelashes and curly chestnut hair smiled that angelic, irresistible smile and said, "Hi Mom."

I walked to the window and looked out. Down below on a lower roof were a plethora of multicolored plastic action figures, soldiers, and other sundry characters all about two inches high, lying in a random pattern achieved as they obviously flew from the open window to their new destination.

Jean-Paul had been playing with his friend a short while earlier in his room, and one of them had to be the culprit. "Jean-Paul," I asked. "Did you throw the men out the window?" Nothing. I could not assume he did or did not do it. I had to hear the words from him myself. "I promise you, nothing will happen if you tell me the truth," I said.

"You promise?" he asked timidly.

"Yes," I said.

"I did it," he confessed.

Perhaps he thought the wrong was littering or not taking care of his toys. It was not that. It was that with his admission my heart froze. My mind and my body shook with the realization that not only could he have fallen through the window that day, but since he had the propensity to see things fly through the window, he could fall through in the future.

So I did not keep my promise. I don't remember the punishment. It may have been a spanking or some personal deprivation. I had to tell him how serious this was and how scary this was to me.

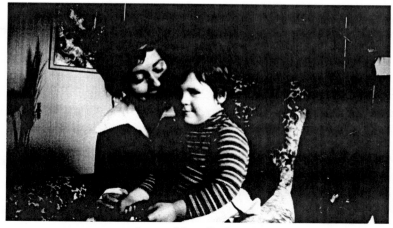

Joan and Jean-Paul, 1975

Joan with Jean-Paul's family, 2008

Jennifer, Jean-Paul and Joan, 2008

Joan and Jean-Paul, 1991

Now, at thirty-five, Jean-Paul tells that story in a light-hearted manner—that I convinced him to confess and did not keep my word.

He is an excellent father to his seven-year old daughter, Ariana, and five-year old son, Liam. His son is so much like him in looks and manner. Parenting styles are different now than they were before. There is no spanking. There is explaining and teaching a lesson. What would you do in the same circumstance, Jean-Paul?

This much I know. Being a father, he has to understand that my discipline came from love and not from anger. It came from protectionism. It came from trying to control the future.

Even today, I would have had to make the same decision.

Joan's note: "Written on Yom Kippur, the Day of Atonement"

(October 9, 2008)

From "Not Giving Up [1]"

Let go and let God take over.
Lord, purify my soul and mind and fill me with your grace and love.
I am missing Jean-Paul already and he is still here.
I love him so much.

He is such a source of strength and support for me.
I thank him for giving me this week so beautifully.

(May 26, 2009)

Rain

When my son, Will, graduated from Harvard in 2002, it was the first time in thirty years that, rather than a bright shining day smiling down on those accomplished men and women, it rained. Actually, it poured so hard that eventually everyone left the convocation space, the place that required a ticket for entry and over an hour to pass through security, a consequence of our new society after 9/11. We walked back to his Harvard residence, Dunster House, in streets filled with three inches of water.

When Will graduated from MIT Sloan in 2008, I looked forward to a nice sunny day. However, history did repeat itself. As we stood in line to pass through the security check to enter our tickets-only seats, the heavens truly opened up. Luckily, the school had the foresight to stock saran-wrap like ponchos. One had to traverse the campus to find the tent that was distributing them, but, once obtained, the poncho was a miracle worker. The audience was a sea of plastic-wrapped parents, family, and friends, hardly moving, raindrops glistening. It did stop raining eventually during that three-hour commencement, and we warmed up under our plastic incubation tents.

When we had a heat wave this week and our air conditioning was blown by a power surge, the most welcome sound was the thunder and lightning preceding the rain. The rain was a blessed rain, bringing relief from the heat. Open the windows and feel the cooler air come in. How comfortable to listen to the sound of the rain on the roof when I am cozy in bed.

Rain.

(June 14, 2008)

From "Every Week is a Fresh Start"

Today marks a new set of visitors, as Will and Sarah arrived this morning. Will and Sarah are delightful to be with, and I am so happy that they are here.

I believe this week will be challenging but good. We will write every day and talk and share. We will get some projects accomplished, writings typed, photos organized, Alaska book completed. I will look forward to enjoying every day, living in the moment, appreciating the flowers, nature, and warmth and caring of family and friends.

Can I convince Will to put some flower essence on my feet once I am in bed? I am happy for a deep, peaceful sleep tonight, free from pains and strange dreams. I will embrace the healing powers of sleep and rest.

(July 3, 2009)

Visits from Children

It is March 15, 2008
Alyssa has come to visit for a week
Will has come to visit for the weekend
What a wonderful gift they are; such wonderful children
We had a good time having dinner, talking
      and watching the movie *Michael Clayton*

Today, March 16, Alyssa and I did Tai Chi and then
Alyssa led us in the most wonderful yoga class
Tonight we are going to the Darien High School production
      of *The Music Man*

(March 18, 2008)

Will and Joan during a summer in France, 1983

Joan with Will and Sarah, 2008

Joan with Will and Sarah, 2009

Joan dancing with Will at his wedding, 2004

From "Notes from my Children"

Will's thought for the day: *You've accomplished the end of radiation. You've accomplished something that seemed impossible only a few weeks ago. With your strength and conviction, anything is possible.*

Alyssa writes often beautiful and encouraging cards, strengthening our bond and even more reminding me of how close we are. The hummingbird in her garden reminds her of the blue and red birds in mine. We are always connected heart and soul. That is true. Her admonition of keep being strong and enjoying every day is true. I know it could be easy to give up, but I won't. I will do it for her, for me, and for whatever beautiful events may blossom in the future. I am surrounded by love and prayer. I consciously open my heart to receive all these prayers.

In Will's thought for the day, he reminds me that I finished radiation, something that would have been very difficult a few weeks ago. With my strength and conviction, anything is possible. I am carrying that banner high, waving it in the sun. I am planting it in my garden for one and all to see.

Thank you dear, sweet children.

(July 20, 2009)

"The ones you love are life's most precious gifts."

Nana

What a joy to be a grandmother, a Nana
Each grandchild is so special, a gift from God
But there is a special allegiance with the first born,
    just as there is with the first-born child
To re-experience all those "firsts" again

As the grandchildren grow,
    what joy in their different personalities
What awe to look into their eyes seeing emotions
    of love, mischief, and frustration, depending on the moment
What a gift to see their smiles light up a room
How easy it is to love each one unconditionally

(December 14, 2008)

Aidan, Adalynn, Johan, Liam, and Ariana in Lake Tahoe, 2006

Grandchildren

Three little darlings
Each one with a distinct personality
Adorable, charming, and challenging
What fun to spend time with each one

The patience required with my children is still required for them
It comes easier
It comes joyfully
I am not the disciplinarian
I am not the schedule maker
I am just the unconditional lover

(November 14, 2008)

Joan and Michael with Liam, Aidan, and Ariana in New Canaan, 2005

A Poem for Ariana from Nana

The grass is turning green
Purple and yellow crocuses are flowering on the lawn
The birds sing at morning's first light
    announcing a new day
Robins, sparrows, and chickadees are making nests
The woodpecker is signaling for a mate
    rat-a-tat-tat rat-a-tat-tat
Soon the trees will start budding
    unfurling their green leaves
Spring is coming to Connecticut where Nana lives

(April 7, 2009)

Joan with Ariana soon after she was born, 2001

Aidan at Cove Island

Last week when I knew I had time between appointments, instead of the mad dash home to do a few household chores like folding laundry, I decided instead to bring along my sneakers and use that free hour to walk at Cove Island on "the Sound" in Stamford, Connecticut. I had not been there in many years if at all, so it was a new discovery. I walked along the gravel path which runs along the channel where boats are docked. Where row after row of white gleaming boats, sails carefully rolled, are waiting for perhaps one last outing. When I saw the beach at the end of the channel, I could not resist walking on it. There it struck me that when my grandson, Aidan, visits in a few days, I will bring him here, to Cove Island. I continued to walk, discovering many paths and a wide beach. What a great place for him to ride his new razor scooter we have waiting for him. What an opportunity for this landlocked Colorado boy to glimpse the ocean.

When Aidan did arrive, that is exactly what we did on Monday. We took my same exact route with me on foot and Aidan on scooter. We passed the boats and behold he was attracted by that same beach at the end of the channel. Once we left that spot and continued on, behold his next step was exactly where I had to walk and look at the horizon and after that the exact spot I went to look in the water. Could it be — yes, it seemed to be — that I walked with the eyes and wonderment of a six-year old child.

(September 25, 2008)

From "Relief"

There will be no need for oxygen tonight.
My step is lighter coming into the house.

Aidan opens the door and says,
"You look so much better, Nana. You have color in your face."

Out of the mouths of children come the essential truths.
 I believe him.

(May 29, 2009)

Joan with Aidan in New Canaan, 2009

A Poem for Liam from Nana

Our visits together are special and packed with activity
Playing games and cards
Drawing pictures and painting
Making cookies
Preparing dinner and going out for dinner
Going to soccer and hockey games
Listening to piano recitals

Playing outside in the deep, deep snow in Nederland
Making snowmen and sledding
Taking walks along Boulder Creek
Visiting the balloon man on the Pearl Street Mall
Going to the beach in Lake Tahoe
Digging for clams on Bainbridge Island
Spending Thanksgiving in New Canaan
Celebrating Christmas in Boulder

And at the end of the day, when all is done
Sitting on the couch, talking about the day
And reading stories to each other

(April 7, 2009)

Joan with Liam in Boulder, 2008

My Day

I like to run and laugh and play
Everyday is a special day.

I like to ride my bike and play ball
I just want to do it all.

School is such fun, reading and math
At the end of the day I take a long bath.

And when I go to bed and turn out the lights
I dream of adventure and of pirates and knights.

(April 7, 2009; written by Joan for Liam to read out in school)

Joan with Ariana and Liam, 2007

What I Want

It's the Christmas season, and I want this year to be the most memorable it can be. I am not saying that this Christmas will outdo some spectacular ones we've had in the past. Like the Christmases spent at Val d'Isère when we lived in France when our children were so much younger than they are now. Yes, I remember the quaint town, the little church where the priest gave each of us a piece of chocolate as we left mass, where the snow was dazzlingly bright and deep and we skied from morning to night.

Yes, there have been some spectacular Christmases when the brightly wrapped presents circled our large Christmas tree, adorned with colored lights and handmade ornaments, and practically overflowed into the next room.

This Christmas, 2008, will be the most treasured gift for me because I am here to celebrate it together with my loved ones, all of them: my husband, my children, my grandchildren, and Laird, Lisa, Jennifer, and Sarah. I want everyone to absorb the love I feel for them as well as the joy and promise of this season. Yes, we have our stocking gifts and secret Santa gifts, but I want the dearest gift to be a hug, a look, a touch, a sharing of laughter, a sharing of oneself.

I want to feel love, contentment and gratitude zinging around the room we are in.

I want to celebrate life together.

(December, 2008)

Café Gratitude

One of my questions, actually the most important question, especially when I am feeling discouraged, lonely, or bored, is "What am I grateful for?" I owe the genesis of that question to a visit to my daughter in California both this summer and last year. Last year she took me to Café Gratitude, a vegan restaurant with an incredibly imaginative menu. Everything on the menu is prefaced with a reason to be grateful. So that lasagna made out of zucchini noodles and a sauce of thickened cashew milk and filled with tomatoes and vegetables was called, "I am fulfilled," and a green juice drink was called, "I am energized," and so on for every single item which included curries, grains, soups, and desserts. The waiter also usually asks you what you are grateful for.

Sitting outside in a walled-off area on a dirt floor on rough-hewn tables and stools surrounded by trees and birds, I am thinking now how grateful I am to be here, to experience this peace, this love, this simplicity, this kindness, and, of course, this incredibly special time with my daughter. I always bring back with me a Café Gratitude bag full of dark cacao powder, filled with healthy antioxidants and healthy chocolate. I may be delusional about the chocolate, but I am grateful for it. And since I don't drink caffeine, the chocolate may be my energy booster as well. This summer, in addition to the chocolate, I brought back a round orange ramekin and inside are the words, "What are you grateful for today?" I keep it on my kitchen counter where I see it every day, and even if I don't consciously answer the question, I believe that on a subliminal level it keeps me on track.

Last week on a low day, I had to consciously enumerate what I am grateful for, and I realized that there are so many things: my husband, my home, my bed, the peace and beauty of my backyard, my children with whom I speak several times a week, and my grandchildren who accept me as I am and who do love me.

I am grateful that I can look vanity in the face and say you have had your day. It's not that I don't keep trying to look good, but it takes so much more time and work. Yesterday, a successful shopping trip to Talbots in Greenwich lifted my spirits. Luckily, there are clothes that will fit and look nice and make me feel good. I may not, and probably will not, become again the attractive mother of the groom I was in 2004 with straight sheath spaghetti-strapped sequenced top, luxurious hair.

But here I am four years later, rediscovering myself and loving life for what it is.

(September 8, 2008)

CHAPTER 5 –
"BABY STEPS": WORKING THROUGH ILLNESS

I never worried about my cancer or a positive outcome with treatment because I was so fulfilled and happy with my work.

> No matter how ill I feel, I can still pick up my pen and express my feelings, moving them from inside a heavy heart to the freeing words on paper.

In the Spring of 2009, Joan visited Stanford University and met with Stanford Lecturer John Tinker, who invited Joan to contribute a chapter to his forthcoming book entitled, Celebrating Life after Cancer Diagnosis. Over the next few months, Joan corresponded with John, writing and assembling her contribution for the book in the writings that follow. This project meant a great deal to Joan; she referred to it often in her Journal Entries and poems as "The John Tinker Project." She intended her chapter to encourage and educate those diagnosed with cancer on the choices they have for telling their employers and co-workers, for attending to health issues while working full-time, and for deciding when to stop working. Most of all, she wanted to pass along the message that writing through illness can help a person keep going, "baby step by baby step."

CANCER DIAGNOSIS BEFORE EMPLOYMENT

The Moment of Diagnosis

I was diagnosed with breast cancer at age 52 at the end of law school.

I actually received the phone call with the diagnosis right before my very last class of the semester. I was shocked. I had a husband, four children, the youngest child was in the eighth grade, and a new career ahead of me. I remember coming home right away after that phone call. My youngest son, Will, was at home. I told him the diagnosis and that I would be fine, and I believed it. My son put his arms around me and hugged me and said, "You will be fine, Mom."

From that moment, I was focused on studying for exams, graduating, and preparing for the bar exam. My husband was the contact with family and friends and told them what was happening. I did not want to talk about it except with my medical team. I asked many questions and they were straightforward with me.

The Support of Others

I confided in a friend, Elaine Harris, who helped and encouraged me that I would survive. "Just take it one day at a time," she said. "Baby step by baby step."

I had surgery, and then I took my exams and graduated. I started chemotherapy while studying for the bar exam. Often I was too ill to attend the class in person; one of my classmates would bring me a video of the review, and I studied at home.

DECISIONS ABOUT TELLING WORK ABOUT CANCER

My First Employer

I did pass the bar exams for New York and Connecticut, was sworn in as an attorney in both states and ready to start working as an attorney. My first job was as an elder law attorney in Stamford, Connecticut, working for a sole practitioner. I did confide my medical situation and worked conscientiously to show that I could handle the work well, meeting with clients and visiting Medicare offices. However, my employer was not at ease and was always worried about my health and my prognosis. The following spring, after undergoing additional surgery, I was laid off. I knew that this was wrongful termination and was legally actionable, but I did not pursue it because my focus was on the positive: doing well, being happy.

My next job was in White Plains, New York, as an estate attorney, again for a sole practitioner. My employer knew of my health situation so that I was able to leave for radiation treatments. I worked there for two and a half years. Feeling healthy and healed, I looked for a more challenging and supportive position.

Being Hired without Disclosing my Health Situation

I found a new position in Stamford, Connecticut, in a well-known estate planning law firm, Blair & Potts. I loved working there, with the client contact and challenging work. After working for the estate planning law firm for about three years, I shared my health situation with the partners in the firm. At that time, I was cancer free, but I wanted them to know how I could focus despite sometimes overwhelming challenges.

Disclosing to Co-workers and Clients

To share or not to share with my co-workers and clients, especially when there is a recurrence of cancer or when cancer becomes a chronic disease—that was a key question of mine.

I had a good rapport with the clients, even the difficult ones, and credited my life experience for this talent. When, eight years after my original diagnosis, I had a small regional recurrence which required chemotherapy, my employers were very supportive. They left it to me whether I wanted to share my situation with my co-workers as they believed my privacy and comfort level was most important. I did share with my co-workers, telling them that I had to have treatment and would recover. However, I did not share with my clients for professional reasons. I dealt with grieving families who had lost loved ones, some to cancer. I could have great compassion and understanding for them. I did not feel nervous for myself, nor did I want their sympathy for me which I felt would alter the attorney-client situation. This approach worked very well for me.

Work was a focus even when having treatment. My clients never knew, even when I was wearing a wig. I never worried about my cancer or a positive outcome with treatment because I was so fulfilled and happy with my work.

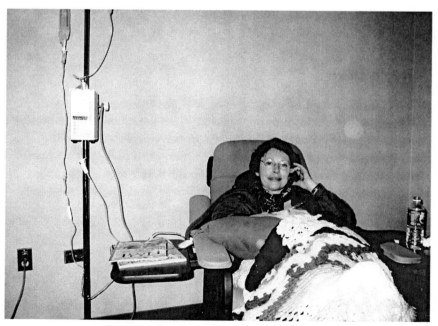

Joan receiving chemotherapy treatment, 2003

NOT WORKING CHANGES THE CANCER EXPERIENCE

Retirement

I retired from the law firm after nine years of working there. I realized (after an intervention by my children asking me to consider to retire so that I would have more time for myself) that I should relieve myself of stress and have more time for healing and more time with my family. I have not missed my job at the law firm and have moved on to other pursuits.

Vulnerability

Although I left on my own terms, my cancer now focused more of my attention. I acknowledge that I am vulnerable, and I turn and form this emotion in a manner that is good for me. I recognize my gift of perseverance, of self knowledge, of what my character really is. I personally acknowledge cancer and live with it. I acknowledge that my cancer has become a chronic disease.

Turning Point

We eventually reach a turning point. We age, we become more fatigued, or the cancer is more serious. What we can control is how we shape our turning points. I had to make the experience of having cancer be good for me. I did not miss work, but I realized that I must focus on other things while I can still do them. By true acceptance, sharing, and hope, I give inspiration to myself and those around me.

MY COPING TIPS FOR WORKING THROUGH ILLNESS

1. **Yoga:** I practice yoga. My practice has declined from leading the class to now doing yoga in a chair or standing up leaning on a walker due to lymphedema (swelling of the limbs). But I accept this.

2. **Tai Chi:** Tai Chi involves gentle movement and can be done in any room. It gives the mind focus, moves your energy, and gives peace.

3. **Family:** I am blessed with family and travel to visit them while I am still able. Now I've reached the point where they must visit me. Being a grandmother, a Nana, is a precious gift. Sharing the day with my children in their home is likewise a blessing. My family is an integral part of my support team. My husband is my chief caregiver. Caregivers need recognition, acknowledgement, and support for their efforts which are both physical and emotional. I use my writing to offer a tribute and thank you to him.

4. **Writing:** I try to write every day. I want to leave some part of me with my family. For Christmas I gave each of them a collection of my 2008 stories and copies of my 2008 watercolors. I am leaving a legacy for my children and grandchildren.

HOW WRITING AFFECTS MY EXPERIENCE OF CANCER

What I Write

I don't specifically experience cancer as having a meaning that describes and gives shape to my writing, neither do I experience writing about cancer as a means of giving cancer a meaning that affects my experience of myself as a person with cancer. Rather there is another relationship between writing and cancer that these questions don't identify. My writing is an exploration of a feeling, an experience or writing prompt that I give myself.

Although I have had cancer for fourteen years, I only started my creative writing last year, in 2008. Up until then, I was an attorney; from the time of my diagnosis until I retired in 2007, my writing was concerned with legal writing. I did keep notes on the names of my chemotherapy and dates of treatment, and even after all these years the facts are imprinted on my mind. I also have a copy of my doctors' notes and keep copies of all tests, CT scans, and PET scans. I also have summarized my medical history on a spreadsheet.

The Purpose of Writing

With the encouragement of my daughter, Alyssa, I started to write, especially when visiting my children in Colorado and California. I wrote short poems and reflections, many of which are now in this book.

In May 2008, I was invited by the Knights and Dames of Malta to go on a pilgrimage to Lourdes, France. I wrote and published a piece about my experience there.

Most of all, I recognize how important it is to live in the moment.

THE BENEFIT OF WRITING

Joining a Writing Group

In 2008, I joined a writing group of excellent writers led by a published author, Drew Lamm. We would listen to poems, write for 40 minutes, and then share our writing. It was the first time I had shared what I wrote. Our leader only commented on the positive details, never criticized. It was then I realized how important it is to read aloud what you have written. I was able to share without self-judgment—a gift to myself.

Forming My Own Writing Group

I realized how important it would be for cancer patients and cancer survivors to express their emotions of fear, grief, worry, and hope. Using as a guide a group conducted at Stanford University by Sharon Bray, the author of *When Words Heal* and *A Healing Journey: Writing Together through Breast Cancer*, I started a Healing through Writing group at the Bennett Cancer Center in Stamford, Connecticut.

Using Sharon's books, her method and prompts, and other poems, I facilitated a group of patients at the Bennett Cancer Center. We would meet once a week for two hours. No one in the group had experience writing. We would listen to poetry, perhaps have a writing prompt, and then just put pen to paper and let it take us wherever it would. We would write from our hearts, and the results have been amazing. We write for thirty minutes and then share what we have written. It has changed our lives.

"It's self-healing. There is a lot of strength in their writing ... and to hear them read and the look of surprise on their face when they've read what they've written ... they say, I didn't know I had it in me."

Sharing Writing with Others

As a result, I have shared so many of my writings with my family and friends, empowering them to write also. In putting pen to paper, I have been able to express my deep feelings, freeing them from festering inside. It has both surprised and pleased me. It has pleased me because no matter whatever difficult aspect of my cancer journey I may be verbalizing, I also feel hope, peace, love, and gratitude. That is specifically how my writing has affected my experience of cancer.

Surviving and Thriving Despite Cancer

How did I manage without writing for twelve years of this cancer journey? First of all, I had the focus of working full time, and I practiced yoga several times a week along with daily meditation and monthly massage. Now, I am at the stage where I have retired from work; lymphedema and abdominal edema have restricted my yoga to chair yoga, and my massage is restricted to lymphatic massage. My writing is an essential tool for surviving and thriving.

Since my children have been here during the last few months, we have been writing together and sharing what we have written. My writing group has come to my home to write with me. No matter how ill I feel, I can still pick up my pen and express my feelings, moving them from inside a heavy heart to the freeing words on paper.

(July 2009)

"I am not looking for years down the road as that could be hard in my present condition. I can acclimate to living as I am by surrounding myself with laughter and beauty, faith, hope, and love."

CHAPTER 6

"ENJOYING LIFE FULLY DESPITE CANCER": JOAN'S FINAL JOURNEY

The breath of life sustains me... But lately, I have become short of breath with exertion when my breath is shallow.

(May 11, 2009)

> Hope, faith, peace, and love have filled me. Body, mind, and soul are working together... I am witness to the renewal of life, nature's gift to me. My spiritual advisor is preparing my soul—God's gift to me.
>
> *(June 6, 2009)*

> My soul is purified, I am at peace. I am ready to accept what may come next... I look forward to creating a legacy of words and love.
>
> *(June 12, 2009)*

> I will take it one day at a time as I always have in the past, with trust in God's help.
>
> *(July 18, 2009)*

WRITINGS ON THE CANCER JOURNEY

My Story

What is my own story? Will it have a happy ending or not?

I am sitting next to the decorated Christmas tree in Drew Lamm's house. I look at the metal icicles hanging delicately, and I am reminded of Christmas in my childhood. I hung identical icicles on my parents' tree, preferring the green and silver, then the gold and silver, over the others. The metal icicles are sturdy, but are hung by a fragile thread. Sometimes the thread would break and have to be restrung. With patience it could always be fixed.

Can I be fixed so easily? I have always been sturdy. Do I hang on by a fragile thread? What breaks the spirit most? Is it pain with its unwelcome embrace? Go away, you are not welcome.

(January 22, 2009)

The Journey

I identify with the winged victory poem—with the breastless warrior, a woman who is strong and proud. A woman who is loving because she cannot hide behind her lost breasts. Her heart is exposed. Her heart must shine forth—a bright light, a beacon not only for others but to guide her every day for herself.

One aspect of my daily journey is as the breastless warrior. I am not flat because I have artificial breasts. My biological breasts are gone. They have served their purpose in love and as a mother nursing four children.

In my daily journey, I feel my heart opening as I have never done before. My breaths are deep and long. My heart is opening more and more to unconditional and non-judgmental love. In my daily journey, this is my centering. This is my means of remaining strong because as I give of myself, I renew myself.

There are bumps in the road of this journey. Sometimes the open heart does not give quite as much fuel as I need. I am learning what I need, what I can do and can't do. In that respect, each day is an adventure.

If you asked me before cancer would I have chosen this path, I would say, "Are you crazy?" I would be still practicing law, my mind would be full of to-do lists. But former routines have been replaced by a sense of tranquility and an increased love of fellow man.

My journey makes each day a discovery and that is good.

(September 29, 2008)

Paying Attention

Yesterday, I had a meltdown of sorts. It was a perfect storm. I was feeling ill since Wednesday and worried what might be the cause. I had eaten little all week and hardly anything on Thursday and Friday. On Saturday, I was somewhat better but not yet myself. We were going to a wedding in the afternoon, and I rested for that all morning with my legs wrapped and up the wall so that they would not be swollen from lymphedema and I would fit into my new shoes.

1:30 pm was show time. I started to prepare for the wedding and was looking forward to wearing my newly bought black pant-suit and white satin flowered blouse set off by new flat shoes. Everything should fit even better than two weeks ago when I tried the outfit on in the store since I had not eaten in the past several days.

That is when the perfect storm hit. The legs looked large even after all that care. The pants were tight in the leg. I could not believe it! I got on the scale. After those days of no eating, I had actually gained weight. If there was a medical or common-sense explanation for this, it did not make any difference. I did not want this.

I finished getting dressed, put on my new shoes, and off we went to the church for the wedding. It was a beautiful wedding. Everyone looked lovely, all dressed up and happy for the radiant bride and groom. Then disaster two struck. I realized that my feet were swollen, and I could not walk in these flat new shoes, a half size bigger than I actually wear. So we went home, and I miraculously found an old pair of black heels that worked and then we went to the reception. There I even managed to dance some slow dances, eat sparingly, and thoroughly enjoy the company of friends at this happy occasion.

Sunday I woke up "paying attention" to how I was feeling. I was feeling down, disappointed, lonely, and not so brave. The opposite emotions that usually course through me. I knew this was not good. I am not yet at the point where I voluntarily write about such things. But I recognized the need to reach out and share how I felt instead of just saying I was fine. So I did just that, not in a complaining but rather an open and frank way with my husband, my girlfriend, and my son, Chris.

I then just breathed and paid attention to what they said to me. Each one was understanding. My husband in the quiet way I can always predict, my girlfriend with an offer to look for larger pants and a lunch date, and my son, Chris, with an offer of energy work zoomed into me over the airwaves from Colorado. He said that while I was sleeping, if my body was open to it, he and his friend Erin would do an energy session on me. I don't know yet if they did or what time it may have happened, but I do know that I slept very peacefully during the night and had pleasant dreams. My issues have not gone away, but I can face them in a cheery light today. I had my leg massaged and wrapped. I wrote my story, and I am happy to share it. I paid attention to what was revealed to me from my soul, from my heart, from my angst, and I respected it.

(October 6, 2008)

Survivor

After reading different interpretations of the word survivor, I have an increased appreciation that the word can mean many things to many people. The word comes to the forefront in cancer as it is highlighted in National Cancer Survivor's Day and in the Relay for Life, which takes place around the country. Survivors make the first loop around the track in the relay. A survivor is defined as anyone who has been diagnosed with cancer and is alive. When I was in Bainbridge Island, Washington, this past summer, I was part of the Relay for Life. I was given a survivor t-shirt and a medal was hung around my neck to show that I had survived thirteen years. Every day I wear an article I received at that relay. It is a purple bracelet which says "Hope."

When I reflect on the word survivor, I realize it has crept into the lexicon of our health vocabulary, slowly but surely. The word does not bother me, but it does not adequately describe who I am either. Thirteen years ago I was asked to give a talk at Stamford Hospital on my breast cancer experience. Two other people with different cancers also spoke. I remember telling the audience that I was a warrior and that I would survive. That's putting it in the active tense. Warrior pose in yoga denotes focus and strength. "Survive," the verb, designates action.

I am a warrior who is surviving and thriving, not a passive survivor. But in the global sense I am a survivor too.

May I survive a long time.

(October 27, 2008)

Gratitude [2]

How many times in my thirteen-year journey with breast cancer have I focused and mobilized my resources? In hindsight, I am so grateful for this focus. It made me achieve my goals: take my law school final exams after being diagnosed with breast cancer, graduate from law school one week after surgery, study and pass the New York and Connecticut bar exams while on chemotherapy, and work at my first law firm job while undergoing radiation. My focus was such that my one goal was to become an attorney and work as an attorney.

In the meantime, I knew that the medical treatments, and chemotherapy in particular, were my friends, my allies. I did everything I could to help my body successfully endure these treatments: vitamins, massage, meditation tapes, and relaxing long soaks in a hot tub with lavender oil.

I moved to a law firm I loved. No one there knew I even had cancer until I told them when, after seven years, lymphedema arrived. Telling them was good as it made them supportive. Then, after eight years, a local recurrence, then after eleven years, a new breast cancer, and after thirteen years, another recurrence.

Today, I am not the same eager warrior I was in 1995, and I have had to give up so many things. But, as I look around and see my friends have aged, some have died, children have grown, life has changed for so many people, and I am still here and I plan to keep holding on and enjoying it.

This is the day the Lord has made. Let us rejoice and be glad.

(December 8, 2008)

Living with Lymphedema

Lymphedema control is my daily challenge. I have secondary lymphedema as a result of cancer surgery and radiation. Manual lymphatic drainage followed by compression wrapping was discovered about 50 years ago in Germany, and it is still the gold standard of treatment today. One would think that, similar to advances in cancer treatment, advances would have been made in the treatment of lymphedema. But that is not the case.

I believe the reason for this is two-fold:

1. There is not the demand or focus on lymphedema (no celebrity calling for its attention or fund-raising for research efforts) and

2. Manual lymphatic drainage (MLD) and compression works. However, MLD is time consuming, takes a certified lymphatic massage therapist to be administered properly, and is only truly effective when followed by compression wrapping.

Compression wrapping, in turn, is time consuming to do. Although some people may have mastered the art of wrapping one limb, to self-wrap two or three limbs is nearly impossible, especially if fingers or toes need to be wrapped as well. Then there is the issue of rolling the wraps after each wearing, washing them often, replacing the batting used under the wraps frequently, and taking them with you as a necessity whenever you travel.

What else can be done, especially when all limbs and the trunk is involved? Pumps don't work and neither do diuretics. It is necessary to wear compression sleeves when traveling, the cost of which are not covered by medicare. Living with lymphedema is not easy.

(December 27, 2008)

The Body

My daughter's good friend and Stanford University colleague Christine Alfano lost her sister, Nancy Thompson, to breast cancer on Saturday, January 3, 2009. Nancy, at age 36, left behind her husband and three young children aged five, seven, and nine. Her young vivacious body was not able to eliminate the cancer cells, even with the help of chemotherapy and surgery. Why? How do you not fight for life to see your children grow, graduate from high school, from college, get married and have their own children?

Dying is scary when you are older, but for the young it must be unbearable. You are really just starting to live, to see your life, your family, your hopes, and your joys come to fruition. What did her body need to fight the big fight? I don't know. I hope she wasn't scared at the end, if she knew it was the end, and had peace and acceptance. I hope her children were able to kiss her good-bye, as hard as that sounds.

I had the same diagnosis as the young woman, triple negative breast cancer, but I was 26 years older than she when I was diagnosed. If I had been diagnosed at 36, my children would have been five, nine, and eleven, and my fourth child would not yet have been born.

When I was diagnosed at 52, two children had graduated from college, my daughter was married, my third child was about to graduate college, and my youngest was in the seventh grade. My will to live for them kept me going. One by one wonderful events happened. I saw my son, Will, graduate from high school, then college. I saw my daughter, Alyssa, receive her Ph.D. and my son, Will, his MBA. I saw three grandchildren shortly after they were born and have the joy of sharing in their lives. I achieved my Juris Doctor and acquired a good job as an attorney. I thanked my body for this. I gave it massages, relaxing soaks, yoga stretching, soothing lotions, and relaxation techniques in gratitude and love.

My body guarded me until I was 60 and cancer cells appeared again: conquered, then back at 62, conquered, then back at 63, and now it has been what we call chronic for three years. My body has been hit hard—hair lost, breasts lost, implants lost, body swelling from lymphedema (excess edema as a result of a compromised lymphatic system) causing swollen arms, legs, and feet. My body has lost its beauty on the outside.

I will try to keep loving it, keep nourishing it, keep encouraging it to try new exercises that may help it feel better and move the lymph better. I will keep happy and laugh for my body. Although my body cannot do what it wants or likes to a great extent, there is much it can do to help itself. I am working on that with my body. We will do it. And we will keep loving and hugging and kissing, seeing children and grandchildren and friends, celebrating the good and happy times, being compassionate in times of sorrow. My body and I can do it. We're partners; we've been through a lot before, and we'll come through this latest challenge, and other scary ones, with God's grace and love.

(January 5, 2009, on the death of Nancy Thompson)

The Promise

The cold and dreariness of winter has its own charm. Time to go deep inside and think, analyze, create. What promise will come out of rumination? What rebirth in the spring?

Focus

My whole world is focused on my back. On the incessant throb that radiates there. Can I focus on anything else? There are a million things more important. But they won't come, not today.

The Red Dress

If I had a slinky red dress, I would need a body to go with that slinky red dress. So if I had both a slinky red dress and a slinky body, what would I do? I could put on that dress and dance and dance and dance. I would whirl in pirouettes, with the hem of my red dress flowing. I would slip on my red shoes, covered in sequins, with pointed toes and stiletto heels, and strut around the room. I would want to go out, but where to go? Want to have someone see me, but who? Don't have an answer, so this will be my secret fantasy.

(Three writings from January 22, 2009)

Praise Song for My Day

I am here today writing and not in bed with pain or illness. Instead of a break from chemotherapy, which was anticipated for the end of February, I face the unknown of a new chemotherapy. Watch your attitude, I say to myself. Remember how you always accepted chemotherapy as your friend, not your enemy. It was your ally in healing, and your job was and is to help your body tolerate this drug so you can be healed and maybe even cured. Has it been so long that I am letting hope slip away? No, never. Hold onto hope tightly and believe in it.

Praise song for my day that I will be with my children in California next week. I anticipate the hugs and the sharing, the stories and the laughter, the heart-to-heart talks. We all need to be together. They need to see me, that I am well and strong. I need to hold them near and breathe in their specialness.

Praise song for this day and every day.

(February 9, 2009)

What Now

Ever since I fell down a flight of stairs at age three, with a doll in my arms practically my size who lovingly cushioned my fall, intervening between me and the radiator at the bottom of the stairs, unfortunately sustaining a crack in her skull but luckily sparing mine, I have been cautious walking down a flight of stairs, and thankfully, I have not fallen again. I was able to run up the stairs and ascend the steep grade of a mountain without hesitation, but once in a descent direction, the anti-balance forces slowed me down, and caution and even fear took over.

I remember climbing Camel's Hump in Vermont, a fairly challenging mountain. After a rigorous climb, I reached the summit with my fellow alpinists. Sitting there surveying the magnificent vista of landscape was exhilarating. Eventually, we had to descend. Retracing the same route as the ascent would mean a very steep descent. I was told going down the other side of the mountain was a gentler grade.

That was what we decided to do. However, to reach that side we had to traverse the summit, carefully, one foot in front of the other on a ledge no wider than the width of my hiking shoe. There was no room for anyone to hold my hand and help me across. Once started, there was no stopping, no way back. There was just fierce determination, eyes bulging, staring straight ahead, ligaments in neck taut, tension in shoulders, legs wobbly. Don't look to the right, it was a sheer drop down. Just a few more steps, then the even tougher part stepping around the bend, right foot ankling around, left foot pulled and placed in front. Stay upright, don't lean, keep your balance. Finally there, with feelings of relief, perspiration, weakness. The path widened before me: the path down and back to our car in the parking lot. The estimated three-hour trip down the mountain took me five and a half hours. Yes, the grade was less steep, but it also consisted of fields of smooth boulders. You could only walk on there if you were a mountain goat. I preferred the undignified human way of sliding down on my backside. By the time I reached the bottom, my thighs were aching from forcing my feet to stay on the path, and my legs were like rubber bands.

Fast forward 15 years to today, I could not repeat that feat, nor would I want to. Walking up and down stairs carefully is fine, thank you. But what about sitting in a chair, is that a challenge now, too? A few weeks ago, I fell off my kitchen chair trying to reach one of my vitamins that had fallen on the floor way out of reach. Over I went, just like my two year-old grandchild, Aidan, had done on another occasion.

Then last night, I was just planning to sit at my desk, perching on the edge of my desk chair, which has wheels, while at the same time moving a bag leaning against the desk drawer and opening the drawer at the same time. Everything went into movement. The bag was pushed aside, drawer opened, and the chair rolled back, leaving me suspended in air until I forcefully hit the floor with my coccyx bone. Thump, ouch! Is anything broken? Can I move? Slowly, cautiously, I rose to my feet. I know I will be sore, but another tragedy has been averted.

(March 12, 2009)

Laughter

Yesterday I picked up a book my son gave me called *The Book of Lawyers' Jokes*. I believe I was thirsting for some levity. I reflect on the books I read, and most are serious novels, and the TV shows I DVR and watch each week are weighty in tone: *24*, *Lost, Grey's Anatomy, Damages*, interspersed by some levity from *The Office* and *3rd Rock*. In my daily life I am more solemn than silly, not particularly gifted with the witty one-liner or with a memory for jokes. That is my husband's gift. As a result, he laughs often, a quality that I have come to appreciate more and more as time goes on. My mechanism to lighten up is to release my inner child with all that a child possesses: imagination, trust, joy, hope, anticipation, and laughter. I once attended a workshop called, "Releasing Your Inner Child" at Kripalu Yoga Center in Massachusetts, and it was a turning point for me. I came back a disciple sharing even with my employer and co-workers at my law firm just how good it feels to release your inner child. In this vein, I have had many laughs with friends over something said, a funny movie or play, tears streaming down face, hardly able to breathe.

I don't recall if there was an instance of my personal action being the cause of laughter of many people. I know, however, that I take myself less seriously now and can laugh at an embarrassing situation and even share it.

One such situation occurred when I was working as an attorney in Stamford on Tresser Boulevard in a high rise office building, one of four, located next door to the Marriott Hotel. I was on chemotherapy and wearing a wig. Every day at lunch time, I would go outside and walk around the block once or twice, sometimes with a co-worker and sometimes alone. This particular day it was chilly and windy, my fellow walkers declined, and I went out alone. I wore a baseball cap tightly over my wig and walked with my hand often holding onto the cap. I was in the home stretch, near the corner of Atlantic and Tresser. It was a busy intersection, with many cars lining up for the light to change. All I had to do was round the corner, pass the Marriott, and then enter my office building. The wind had died down and I relaxed, enjoying the last minutes of the walk. Then, a gust of wind came without warning. The next thing I knew, my cap was lying on the sidewalk, a few feet away. I quickly retrieved it. But where was my wig? I looked and looked and did not see it.

Panic! Intuitively, I touched my head and there it was, blown inside out, hanging on perilously by one single clasp attached to the hairs on top of my head. The movement of my hand did knock it off. I picked it up, quickly put it on, then the baseball cap. Avoiding the looks of people in the audience of cars, I quickly made my way to my office building. Was it my imagination that people were staring at me inquisitively? Up I went in the elevator to the tenth floor. First stop, there was the ladies' room. I looked in the mirror and saw the reason for all the stares. I had put my wig on completely backwards!

(March 30, 2009)

"Laughter is the best medicine … It is the balm that soothes the hurt, the frame for the smile; it is a release of a puff of happiness."

Border Crossing

It was moving from day into night, from warmth to cold, from comfort to anxiety, from assurance to disbelief when I was diagnosed with breast cancer fourteen years ago and crossed the border from health to illness.

The diagnosis and subsequent treatment created a different person, a gentler, kinder, more attentive and sensitive person. I took care to listen to my body to nurture it, to rest, to relax.

I acknowledged my support system consisting of my medical team, family and friends who worked with me for my survival and cure. I gave all my attention as a listener and my heart as a friend, wife, mother, and grandmother.

I like this new person. Can I remain this person and cross back over the border to health? Does it matter? We really never go back, but just forward embracing each new day, grateful for each new day. The path is not always smooth. It is not always a grassy field dotted with wildflowers next to a babbling brook, but may have uneven ground with ruts and stones and sharp ascents and descents.

However, the same glorious sun rises and sets and shines over this path. The same moon and stars blanket it at night. The same seasons enfold it, the promise of spring, the warmth of summer, the brilliance of fall and the crystal clear cold of winter. Anxiety and fear are muted.

Acceptance, hope, and faith are companions along with the love and encouragement of my support system. It is my life to model and shape and love each day.

(April 12, 2009)

JOURNAL ENTRIES: MAY TO SEPTEMBER 2009

On May 6, 2009, Joan flew to California to attend Stanford University's Write Retreat at Fallen Leaf Lake, near Lake Tahoe, as a guest of her daughter, Alyssa, who was teaching at the Write Retreat. While in California, the impact of the cancer and lymphedema accelerated dramatically. Joan flew back to Connecticut on May 17, and her life became one of managing day to day until her last day on September 8, 2009. What follows are the entries from her writing journal in which she recorded her words from those precious days.

May 11 – Breathing (with Alyssa)

The breath of life sustains me. Keep breathing, taking slow deep breaths in and out, filling the area of my collar bone to my abdomen with sweet, nourishing breath. Concentrating on breathing facilitates blocking out other thoughts, emotions, and physical sensations such as pain, fear, and anxiety.

But lately, I have become short of breath with exertion when my breath is shallow, my heart is racing, and I am struggling to breathe. Fear and anxiety creep in, requiring my mind to order my body to relax, listen to my breathing, stretch it out, relax more.

At Fallen Leaf Lake in South Tahoe, California, an elevation of 6500 feet, I experienced a breathing crisis caused by the high altitude. There I was having the most wonderful time with my daughter, Alyssa, on a Stanford Alumni Writing Retreat. I had been looking forward to this since she invited me last year. It drew me with a palpable force to focus on May 6, the day of my trip to California, regardless of health challenges and obstacles. I accomplished that.

Sharing the learning space with my daughter, listening to her give fabulous workshops to 50 participants, exceeded all expectations, a gift so precious.

We stayed at the Stanford Sierra Lodge, close to the front desk, the first-aid station, and the dining room. My challenge was walking up the stairs after having attended the workshop sessions one floor below. Shortness of breath is not only absence of deep breathing, it is a gasping, heart pounding, am-I-having-a-heart-attack sensation.

On Saturday, after a full day of breakfast outside on the deck in the sun, four hours of workshops including an exercise writing outside overlooking the lake, lunch outside in the sun with five talented, smart, interesting people, and a one-on-one conference with a poet to guide me in the development of my poetry, the crisis occurred en route to yet another session.

My daughter, always so acutely aware, left the room to find the EMT and hopefully oxygen for me. We left the workshop room, sat at a table in the small gift shop, and Anjya, a young EMT with blond hair, sparkling blue eyes, and a warm and confident smile, arrived, carrying her bag containing a stethoscope, a device to measure the level of oxygen in my blood, and an oxygen tank.

She listened to my breathing and said my lungs were clear: good sign. She measured my oxygen, and it was a little low: 94%. "Would you like some oxygen?"

"Yes, thank you." She placed the tube over my ears, inserted the tube in my nose, and turned on the oxygen. Almost immediate relief.

"I don't have enough oxygen to get you through the night. I strongly suggest you consider going to Urgent Care or the ER, each approximately a twenty-minute drive to South Lake Tahoe. Another option is to leave and drive home."

I was surprised. I wanted a quick fix, and then to go to dinner and to the evening reading. I was planning to start the evening session by reading two of my writings.

"I'll let you be on the oxygen for a while and see how you feel. I'll get the golf cart and drive you to your room so you won't have to walk up the stairs."

The golf cart was a two-seater utility wagon with a large space in back. From its condition, it was obviously used for hauling soil and plants around the camp.

What a coincidence or act of God that at the moment I sat in the cart, Nami, a participant and a physician, was walking by, and, seeing me with oxygen, asked if she could help. "Yes, can you listen to my lungs. I am wheezing and having trouble breathing."

Back at our room, she listened with her stethoscope. "You do have a wheeze. I strongly suggest you go to Urgent Care or the ER and be evaluated. If you want, I can find Jerry. He is an ER doctor also participating in the retreat."

She was back in a few minutes with Jerry to listen to my heart and breathing, and he detected a wheeze on my exhale. "I strongly urge you to go to the ER, let them run some tests—blood, EKG, CT scan, x-ray—to rule out a pulmonary embolism and congestive heart failure. We do not have enough oxygen for more than a few hours. In the meantime, I'm going to have you sit here without oxygen for 30 minutes and then come back to see how you feel and check your O2 level."

There goes our last night's farewell dinner, I thought. He returned. O2 level was 95-96, not bad. Breathing was easier. "Let's go for a walk," he said. That was more difficult, shortness of breath returning somewhat. Again, he stated his reasons for going to the ER, and I countered with all my reasons for not going, all focusing on my complex medical issues. With a final word of caution—"It's too risky not to go"—he left for the evening reading.

I convinced my daughter to go to the dining room and bring us something we could eat for dinner in the room. She went and returned with Tom Barnes carrying the plates of food. Tom, a poet and inhabitant of Fallen Leaf Lake, was a presenter on the retreat. We had had dinner with him the previous night and gotten to know him.

"Thank you. We'll have dinner now," I said.

He did not take the hint to leave but pulled up a stool and sat at the table. "I am a coach and have seen the effects of the altitude on some people. You must leave now, go down the mountain, and you will feel better."

Another God messenger? I thought about it. I was going to miss tonight's and tomorrow's closing activities either way. Going to bed was not going to relieve my symptoms. Going to the ER was not an option I wanted to pursue.

We packed our bags. Tom never stopped talking and never left the room. He helped pack the car and walked me to the car.

We were off, heading down the mountain at 9:30 pm, watching every marker—7300 feet, 6500 feet, 6000 feet, 5500 feet—until an hour later after a winding drive in the mountains, honking the horn to chase away the many deer grazing on the side of the road every few miles, we arrived at sea level and I felt some respite.

Hours later, we finally arrived home again in Mountain View, at my son and daughter-in-law's home, at 2:30 am. Will greeted us at the door, smiling. "I said to come back early on Sunday so we could spend Mother's Day together, but I wasn't thinking of the middle of the night!"

May 14 – Day Trip to Half Moon Bay

After returning to Mountain View from Fallen Leaf Lake on Lake Tahoe early Sunday morning, for many reasons plans were changed from staying with my daughter and son-in-law, Alyssa and Laird, in Half Moon Bay to staying with my son and daughter-in-law, Will and Sarah, in Mountain View. Laird came for dinner every night until he left for his business trip, and Alyssa also moved in with her blow-up mattress in the living room. We are truly enjoying the family time together: talking, laughing, and having meals together. They are all very attentive and kind to me, recognizing, addressing, and helping me with my various health challenges.

Alyssa and I were planning to go to yoga Thursday morning in Half Moon Bay. We had to keep to that plan because a birthday surprise was planned for her after yoga class with the wonderful people in the class. We traveled from Mountain View to Half Moon Bay and arrived at Enso, the yoga studio, with two minutes to spare. We entered the anteroom, took off our shoes and entered the studio. Immediately the warmth of the room and smiles of the class put me at ease. At each person's place was a mat and chair. I had told Courtney, our yoga teacher, that I could only do yoga in a chair now because of my lymphedema and edema. She thoughtfully offered chair yoga to everyone in addition to or as an alternative to work on the mat. Ninety minutes of stretches, twists, and deep breathing nurtured my mind and body. I was transported to a new dimension of peace and tranquility, so warm and sheltered inside the room in contrast to the thick white, cool fog blanketing the ocean and sand outside.

When the class was over, I read my story about the class and the different friends of Alyssa's who came, ending with a tribute to Alyssa, to the wonderful person she is, and there we all were there to celebrate her birthday with much love. Birthday cards were given, tea was served, Alyssa's friend Deb passed around the blueberry muffins she had made and showed Alyssa the flowers and butterfly balloon she bought for her. Such a good friend. She, along with Courtney, our teacher, had helped me organize the birthday surprise. I knew Alyssa was so happy as well as surprised.

The celebration was not yet over. Soup and salad with Deb and Alyssa at Chez Shea, and coffee in Alyssa's garden afterwards completed this wonderful day trip. The garden offered its botanical delights in a wild profusion of color and varieties, violet fuchsia, white and orange roses, white alyssum, purple flowering oriental sage, rosemary, pink hydrangea, white calla lilies, yellow lilies and so many others. In one corner of the garden were two raised beds, newly built and seeded by my son-in-law, Laird. In just a few days, the seeds were germinating, promising lettuce, arugula, varieties of carrots and beans. Don't walk in front of the motion sensor or be sprayed by the cat repellent water gun.

Just as we were leaving, several hummingbirds flew in and hovered over the trees, showering their good luck blessings upon us.

I'll be back, Half Moon Bay.

May 21 – No One Said You Can't Do This Because You Are a Girl (with Alyssa and the Writing Group)

I was an only child of doting parents who wanted me to be happy, never obstructing my view with a constraint of being a woman. But in their dreams, I would be an entertainer; they gave me singing and dancing lessons and the middle name of Marilyn after Marilyn Monroe. I was told that being a secretary would be a great career after high school. When I expressed the desire to go to college, there were no objections, and I was also awarded a full-tuition scholarship to college. I believe that in this way, my confidence and drive to succeed was nurtured. Realizing that I liked science and that women were welcome in science in the late 1960's, I followed that direction.

Although always holding on to my dreams as a wife and mother, I saw that men and women are different and now, after 42 years of marriage, I look back to observe the me I have become: the gradual emergence of a beautiful butterfly from a plodding caterpillar.

I became the giver, the nurturer, living for my husband and then my children happily. Without a second thought, we followed where my husband's career took us: to New Jersey, to New York, to Connecticut, to France. I was and still am so much in love with my husband and my family that they always come first.

And yes, I have had time for my career as an attorney when I was 50. That was important for me, my personal fulfillment, my strength, my personal accomplishment, my profession, and my independence—to guard against emptiness as my children left home and against emotional dependence on my husband. As a young wife, I was not astute enough to know that men and women are so different in their approaches. It took years of discovery to realize that our approach as men and as women were normal. I do want and need to talk about my feelings; he does not. I do need a listener, not just someone to solve the problem.

The years of our journey together with my breast cancer have melded and muted distinct lines of behavior. We became one in this stormy and unknown journey together. Now in this stage of my health challenge, we have become each other's pillar of love and support, knowing that each day and each memory is precious. He is my ultimate caregiver.

Even still, we do have some friction as a man and a woman. He wants to be in charge, to take care of me, to have me not worry about the little things. I am engrained in the aesthetics: everything in its place, the details of where everything is in the house, of what is happening now, of what will happen next. It is my natural habitat, my comfort, as much as his warm embrace and tender kiss. I am trying to let go, to not be bossy or ordering around for his sake and mine, for our continued happiness and growth together, as my way of showing appreciation for all he is to me.

May 23 – Church Music

Michael and I were discussing my funeral this morning for whenever the time comes. Best to be prepared. I am listening to music from St. Agnes, Will and Sarah's San Francisco church, on my iPod. I just love every song on that album. Oh, how nice it would be to have music like that. Then I think of what is available at St. Aloysius in New Canaan, and Ellen Sisson singing "Ave Maria" is nice.

How church music differs from church to church, depending on the music minister. We are lucky at St. A's with ours. I remember the beautiful Taize adoration of the Cross, and music during Lent ending our visit to Taize in France so many years ago. It imprinted a memory in our minds and hearts both visually and auditorally. I see the simple, austere chapel made holy by the reverence of people packed in the room—kneeling, praying, chanting—people of all faiths, bald-headed monks in brown robes, citizens in simple peasant garb from nearby villages, visitors from all over the world all kneeling in reverence or sitting on the austere wooden benches with backs, praying and chanting, a universal prayer of many faiths to one God.

From the serious and austere, there is the joyous church music associated with weddings. All the many chances for processing in and exiting after the vows have been professed. I remember listening over and over and helping Alyssa and Laird, then JP and Jen, and finally Will and Sarah, as they made their selections, each couple choosing different songs, expressing their personality. "Jesu, Joy of Man's Desiring" for walking in and "Trumpet Voluntary" for processing out, among the many selections.

Easter is always one of my favorites, when I join in and sing "Jesus Christ has Risen Today, Alleluia," expressing renewal, rebirth, joy, and promise in the midst of white lilies, bells ringing out, and chimes playing. Christmas is magic, a gift waiting to be opened and cherished. So many songs are poignantly beautiful—"Silent Night," "O, Little Town of Bethlehem," and "Angels We Have Heard on High." At weekly mass on Saturday night or Sunday, each mass offers its own musical menu. Soloists on Saturday evening and Sunday at 8 am, children's choir at 10 am, adult choir at 11:30 am, and teen group at 5:30 pm. Each one has its own allure and beauty.

Now my voice has dropped to a lower register, but once I was a soloist with a lovely soprano voice, singing in grade school, high school, and college, both at school and in the choir. Once I sang out freely and lovely. Now I listen and appreciate. I remember my years in the Ukrainian choir—"hos pu ti pu mil oy"—the somber, recusant sounds of the Byzantine music. As a yogini, I've listened to Buddhist chanting, not exactly church music, but peaceful and meditative in its own right. With all these forms, we give glory and celebrate life now or hereafter.

May 23 – Follow-up on Church Music

After reading our stories to each other, Alyssa and I marveled how we touched so many similar themes at our morning writing session today. We could also speak freely and non-emotionally about my wishes for songs at a funeral mass and my desires for disposal of my personal items. I expressed my joyous realization that I can talk about all of this without feeling scared or nauseous. I will prepare and then it will be done, and I can just enjoy and savor each day I have, each glorious day.

Today I look out the bay window of the family room and soak in the underwater sensation of trees, lush with green leaves, thick forest ripe with foliage, the purple orchids on my window seat that smile and give a touch of perfect color. I am sitting here in the morning writing with my daughter, Alyssa. How wonderful is that.

I hear the footsteps of JP, and then he appears, so strong and fit.

This is the blessing of illness, the comfort of my beloved children.

May 24 – Planting Flowers

My sister-in-law, Patty, is visiting and has brought beautiful flowers, her green thumb, and sense of design for planting in my outdoor pots which will now adorn my patio. I will be able to constantly see these Monet flashes of color and form whenever I am at the kitchen table looking out at the gift of nature rolled out before me. There are germaniums in hues of red, pink, and white, and accents of yellow, white, and purple smaller flowers. I must find out their names.

Patty, my husband's sister and a sister to me, has again bestowed on me on this beautiful day, her labor of love. Thank you, sister.

May 24 – His Second Love

My brother-in-law, Jim, is getting married next week, his second marriage, Shelia having died nearly five years ago. Jim is 74, with white hair and beard, a twinkle in his eye, one who loves telling Irish jokes and singing Irish songs, and the eldest of Beatrice and Maurice O'Brien's nine children. He is a well-known professor emeritus of oceanography and meteorology at Florida State University.

Approximately two years ago, Jim met Kae via an Internet dating service. Kae, in her mid-60's, is tall, blonde, friendly, outgoing with a contagious smile, and a retired school principal. They are a perfect match. Jim fell in love and melted like a love-sick puppy. He and Kae started seeing each other every day, going to the gym, and having healthy meals together alternating at his home and her home.

They now own a beautiful new home, starting their new life together as true newlyweds in new surroundings, facing the future hand-in-hand, with excitement and anticipation. Love is very sweet to them the second time around.

Congratulations, Kae and Jim. We love you and wish you good health and much happiness.

(Joan wrote this to be read out at the wedding, as she was unable to attend)

May 25 – Restless Night

Soft pillow under head had moved, and I was uncomfortable. Dreaming of someone telling me to breathe without oxygen and that my anasarca was stopping the toxins being eliminated took on a tone of reality. I awoke Michael to ask if this did happen, meanwhile asking for the light on in the kitchen, fan on in the room, and some covers removed. I also needed him to hold my hand and sit next to me. My ear was throbbing, and I took Tylenol, actually afraid to take Vicodin. I eventually relaxed and fell asleep, but the pillow moved again, so I awoke early and was up at 6:30 am. For tonight we will know how to arrange it better. I am a little weary and tired and miss Alyssa. I am trying to hang on until she comes back on June 4. In the meantime, JP and Michael are taking good care of me, and both Will and Chris arrive on Thursday, together with Lisa and Aidan. Friday should be an interesting day, as JP is leaving—another traumatic event—and Judy Boughrum will be here.

It is a cloudy day, but the colorful flowers smile at me through the sliding glass window, sparkling pinks, reds, yellows. I am comforted by their beauty. Now the busy day begins—shower, McBrearitys, Father Ian—how we do try to do so much, but there are so many people to see. It is hard to know how I will feel each day.

May 26 – Not Giving Up [1] (with JP)

During my phone conference call tonight with Donnie Yance, my naturopath, he said that I was giving up on surviving when I should not be. There were still protocols I could embrace, chemotherapy that I could take that would keep me going. I admit, when Dr. Bar said to me last week that there was nothing more he could do for me, that my edema and lymphedema would continue to get worse, and that I had a few weeks left to live, I accepted it without a whimper. I was feeling badly. I could not breathe, have over 60 pounds of water weight, and if he could suggest nothing, what could I do? Emails and calls to Dr. Maria Theodoulou at Sloan Kettering were completely unresponsive. She is supposed to be my back-up person, the one with exposure to so many breast cancer patients and to so many trials. Why does she not call? If she concurs with Bar, she should tell me; if she does not, she should tell me. Why is she silent?

There may be nothing to what Donnie said in that it may not work, but it has stoked the fire of hope within me. I always have hope—hope for a beautiful day, beautiful moments with my husband and children. I am not hopeless. But now I have the hope of exploration of possibility, acknowledging the reality that it very well may be as Bar has said and preparing for that. I plan to continue with my priorities—writing my final chapter, preparing my stories for publication to my children, writing my letters, seeing my friends, meeting with Father Ian, preparing my soul, accepting my humbleness of dependence on others with gratitude and grace. This is my opportunity to practice patience and be compassionate and understanding to my loved ones.

From the energizer bunny in the morning to a weakened battery at noon, I know they are correct in the schedule they have prepared for me. I love them so much for it.

How can I temper my frustration? Well, it is not necessary. It is another burden that can be cast aside, something that does not matter in light of all the other wonderful activities I have on my list. Let go and let God take over. Lord, purify my soul and mind and fill me with your grace and love.

I am missing Jean-Paul already and he is still here. I love him so much. He is such a source of strength and support for me. I thank him for giving me this week so beautifully.

I love my husband—his caring ways, his smile, his love. I am blessed with my People of God. This is the day the Lord has made, let me give thanks and be glad.

I don't know what will happen in the near future. Fear comes into this uncertainty. My challenge is to go bravely each day with happiness. With God's help I can do it.

May 27 – How Does It Feel to be Told I Have Two Weeks to Live? (with JP)

I hear it but I don't feel it. I am numb. I do not cry. I do not scream. I do not despair. I ask questions and plan my next steps. I tell Bar I want to drain the fluid from around my lungs and around my heart. He says he wouldn't do anything, but he agrees. Luckily for me, I did that because I found out there is no current tamponade or imminent tamponade, which would have caused the heart to collapse and the blood pressure to drop, at least for now. As Bar said today, the one life-threatening situation has been removed. And the fluid drained from the lungs giving tremendous relief for about two days. But I still have the tremendous pressure of the lymphedema and anasarca. So the deadline for living so to speak has not changed in my mind.

With the help of Alyssa and Jean-Paul, who immediately came to visit and stayed, I was able to talk about end of life issues. Michael and I talked about funeral arrangements. I wrote a list of priorities I want to achieve, among them leaving a legacy of my writings—a 2009 book of writings—perhaps also including some new watercolors.

I have not changed my mind, even though now perhaps the situation means more than two weeks, but we never know. I have to still prepare as if that were the situation. Following good intentions are like walking on a tightrope; a distraction can make you fall off. Jean-Paul and Michael have been handling my schedule, my visitors and naps and writing time. How will my priorities be impacted if I add in daily radiation—trips to the Bennett Center for 10 days?

How will my priorities be affected if I don't radiate and develop cellulitis or infection or serious pain? If I do nothing, I may have two weeks, but then I might need hospitalization which I don't want. One part of me says trust in God and just let it be. Another part is saying God is speaking to you through Dr. Bar for radiation and Theodoulou for etoposide.

God has given me the strength and will to carry on with a fire within me, as JP said. I will let it rest for tonight and offer it in prayer, and I know and believe the correct answer shall be revealed.

May 28 – Rejuvenation (with Will and Chris)

Today I danced with my narcotic, morphine, to combat my lack of oxygen sensation. One dance was fine. Giving him a second shot, he turned on me with a vengeance so that I was emotionally exhausted and physically sick. I knew I could ride him out, and I did. The next time we waltz, we will keep our distance. I've learned that lesson.

I looked with food envy at the eggplant rollatine, tortellini with porcini mushrooms, and green beans that Susan Goodman brought over. I did have one of her delicious whole wheat raisin rolls with pumpkin seeds and some chicken broth, which this evening was perfect.

Then at 7 pm the magic happened. All of our women's group came over—Sue Lione, Sue Scannell, Sue Reen, Sue Goodman, and Maggie Pierce—and our missing two, Merrily Krauser and Mary Lee MacDougall, joined us via Skype from Florida. Will and Chris, both here together, provided technical expertise and filled in details to ease my talking too much. What a gift to have such close friends whom you know love you and care for you so much, with whom I can be myself, not worry about how I look, and the real me can shine from inside to the outside. I was buoyed as if drifting in a cloud in the lightest blue on a gently sunny day. Champagne was poured, my favorite: Veuve Clicquot. Dare I take a sip after my stomach somersaults of the afternoon? I tentatively put my lips to the glass and sipped the delicious bubbly. It felt right. Besides, the French say it is the best cure for an upset stomach.

In the space of a few hours, I am rejuvenated. I have Will taking over the schedule control with his laughter and enthusiasm and plans.

Everything is going to be fine.

May 29 – Decision for Next Step

VP-16, the oral chemotherapy which CVS is still trying to get from the warehouse, has been suggested by Dr. Maria Theodoulou and Donnie Yance, hoping that it would combat the cancer in the lymph system and relieve some of the anasarca and perhaps also the ear. Bar said that it is an old chemotherapy working on a different mechanism than I have had before. He has no idea or proof if it will work or not work. He advocated instead having radiation done on the ear because he sees that as the most imminent problem and as a worse case can lead to cellulitis. I originally thought that I would do the radiation first, get the ear under control, and then start the chemotherapy. The chemotherapy carries risk of nausea, low blood count (especially hemoglobin) and definite hair loss. Will made the excellent proposal to have the chemotherapy first. Who knows, it may work to help everything. Whereas the radiation would help only the ear, and also there is the burden of going to the Bennett Cancer Center every day for eleven days and having to lie down, the chemotherapy would require a weekly visit for a CBC, and perhaps that could even be done by the visiting nurse at home. It sounds like a persuasive argument to me.

Right now, I don't care. I have been here in the ER for hours waiting for Dr. Stepp and having a pleural effusion—fluid drained from the lungs. I am hungry—no starving—and I want to be home, where Lisa and Aidan are and where my friend, Judy Boughrum, is. Luckily, Michael and Chris and Will are here with me.

Patience and hope have fallen into a bucket deep in the well. There is a long rope to pull it out, and I am sure I will later, but it is looking bleak right now. Another reason to stay away from hospitals. Can we ever get this show on the road?

May 29 – Relief

It's done. The needles are in, the fluid is flowing out. I am sitting on the side of the gurney, legs dangling over, hospital gown opened in back, arms draped over a food tray. A white pillow and my Japanese pillow are placed on top. I rest my head in a yoga restorative pose and breathe. The only wince from my body is when the needle goes in with the numbing medication—right side, then left side. I close my eyes. My thoughts drift. I start dreaming I am sitting on a rose-colored blanket behind a goat's head. The goat sits underneath me, legs spread out. He moves his head gently and does not disturb me. Someone says something, and he is gone. Back to breathing and relaxing—in and out, out and in, over and over until I start to cough. Then I know most of the fluid has been drained. Ease and relief of breathing spread over me with the knowledge that this is a precious moment, like a rare beautiful diamond you can hold only for a while. The fluid will come back; other measures must be taken. But for tonight, I enjoy, I savor. There will be no need for oxygen tonight.

My step is lighter coming into the house. Aidan opens the door and says, "You look so much better, Nana. You have color in your face." Out of the mouths of children come the essential truths. I believe him.

My celebratory dinner is waiting—filet mignon, courtesy of Frank and Ellen, Stag's Leap Merlot, courtesy of Alyssa and Laird. The smiling faces of Michael, Will, and Chris surround me. They were with me; they are relieved. They can celebrate too, with flank steak, not quite filet.

We are one in this journey tonight, and it had the perfect ending.

May 30 – Celebrating the Ordinary (with Chris and Will)

Sitting on the porch, feeling the warm breeze waft through the room through the open sliding doors, looking at the beautiful array of flowers on my patio—red germaniums, pink germaniums, blue, yellow and purple flowers purchased and planted by Patty and Jean-Paul, and a very large plant of light purple flowers with a dark center, a gift from friends, and sitting next to Chris while he was reading to me from *Siddhartha*, I thought, what a glorious day. I am breathing easily today after having the fluid drained yesterday. If we could magically drain the interstitial fluid, I could go back to where I was a few weeks ago: still interacting, driving, traveling. Wishful thinking does not make it happen. Today I had a new normalcy of breath, sweet luxurious breath without labor. Sweet luxuriant breath, sweet as honey, opulent like silk, smooth as velvet.

I listen to the sound of the birds. The second tenants are moving into the birdhouse on the patio. The beautiful bluebirds with orange breasts have left. The cardinals have left. I have not seen nor heard any babies. Perhaps they are nesting and hatching on the branch of a tree or in the large rhododendron bushes lush now with lavender flowers. The little industrious brown bird has spent most of the day bringing long twigs to the round hole of the birdhouse. Sometimes she turns just perfectly so the twig fits in. Other times she tries and tries and flails and fails, and then tries again. That is her normalcy and it is mine too. Keep trying—keep going.

I don't have to know what day it is, what time it is. I have my guardian angels directing me, arranging my schedule. My day flies so fast. No newspapers are read, no news is watched—so different for me, an aberration of my normalcy.

But my children are visiting and that trumps all. Normalcy is a new path through a golden wood of light.

I am led down this happy, carefree path. I trust and I hope. I have faith in those I love.

May 31 – Balance

When I was a mother of young children, I balanced my household chores with taking care of the children, playing with them, stimulating and encouraging them along with my personal desire for personal enrichment, whether it was volunteer work, taking an adult education class in the evening, or painting with the children during the day.

When I was in law school, the balance shifted perhaps too much to my studies. I was obsessed. I felt I had one shot at this course of study and wanted to do well. Michael did the shopping and cooking and went to Will's sport games. If I was not in school, I was always at home, studying upstairs, and I could see them or they me whenever we wanted. Was this one-sided balance detrimental to me? The litigation clinic was a constant source of stress, being expected to perform as in a top-notch law firm while at the same time studying for classes. Taking contract law when I never even had economics and being awarded the highest grade in that course. But that was fine. And being an editor on the law review was good, even if much work. The litigation clinic and litigation class were my nemesis. Did I make myself sick? Did I weaken my immune system that the cancer cells were able to attack? Sometimes I wonder about that. But one can't look back, only forward.

Having breast cancer taught me to strive for better balance—to balance my career with taking good care of my body—yoga, massage, meditation, and visualization, and of course family life—so very important. How enjoyable were the concerts, sports games, and sharing in the changing lives of my children. I often spoke of balance with my co-workers, how important it was and how I constantly strove to achieve it.

Now that is all behind me. My balance challenges are micro, but still important, still challenging. How to balance my priorities, what I want to achieve with what time I have—writing, painting, reading, exercising with chair yoga, treadmill, Tai Chi. I haven't done Tai Chi in weeks. Why not? It needs to go on the schedule. My best intentions don't always translate into action. Most of all is family. That is what I want most—to be close and near to my loved ones. Not to demand it, but to appreciate and love it when it is here.

If there is a reward in life for trying to be the best mother I could be, it is being with my children as adults and with my husband as we have become seniors together, still in love.

June 1 – Working with Disability

Among the many new people who came to the house today—day nurse, night nurse, afternoon caregiver—was a physical therapist, Jean Meyer. She evaluated the situation and praised us for work well done. Then she set in to correct how it really should be done. The goal is for me to use my arms and my own weight to lift me out of chair, out of bed, off the toilet. It means new accessories—a walker instead of a cane for balanced walking, a raised commode with chair rails, an electrical chair that tips forward and enables you to get out. As much as I want to move under my own power and not be totally dependent on someone to get me up from a chair, the toilet, the bed, I am taken aback by these "handicapped" accessories. I hadn't added 2+2 and arrived at 4. I didn't like the way they look or what they mean or stand for.

But here I am—another threshold to be crossed to help me conquer this particular battle. So I know deep in my heart I will do all that is necessary. Except I must keep the aesthetic beauty of my home and not turn it into a hospital. I believe with creativity that can be accomplished. If it helps me and my caregivers, it must be done.

June 2 – Remembrance

Losing your best friends when they die is a wrenching experience— Dottie Wiele to ALS, Kathy to pancreatic cancer, and Nancy Thompson to breast cancer. As difficult and sad as these experiences are, it is an uncertain and somewhat scary situation when you are facing the possibility of your death perhaps sooner than later.

I remember all the years when some people didn't even know I was having chemotherapy, since I was working, traveling, and socializing. Then, just in the past few months, the lymphedema increased, and in the past few weeks the abdominal edema increased. But the hardest of all is the difficulty in breathing because of fluid that accumulates in the pleural sac under the lungs and so far has been drained twice, giving immediate relief like a miracle. I have enough oxygen. But my brain thinks it is air deprived. I am doing my best yoga breathing and relaxation to control and ease my breath. My family, friends, and children are so compassionate and supportive. I have attentive caregivers. I am meeting with a priest, Father Ian, and we talk about the next life. I still need more talks; that is for sure.

I love looking out at the lush greenery, the colorful flowers in all hues of color. I love seeing people, and I am planning to leave a legacy of my writing. To share some of who I am by putting it down on paper where it can last forever. I still have faith, hope, love, and gratitude for all my blessings. Father Ian says that my soul is being purified at this time and that I am making saints of those who come to visit because they are carrying out acts of mercy. This is the mystery of life and death, perhaps enfolded in trust and faith.

June 3 – Trust, Faith, and Guidance

Meeting a new doctor that you trust with your care is a positive situation when you believe him to be sincere, smart, and honest with you. Dr. Timothy Hall is such a man. I need to trust and believe he will take care of me tomorrow, and I will listen to my bedtime pre-op meditation to relax my body and to visualize all going according to plan. We will do our part, and they will do their part, and all will be well. I will have Michael, Will, and Alyssa with me for strength and courage. Afterwards, I may have some blessed relief in time for celebrating 67, God willing. Then I will return home to my beautiful, comfortable home, my gorgeous flowers, my yard, my comfortable rooms filled with the love of family and friends to help me. Father Ian supported my faith tonight. I must trust in my doctors and in my body's responses and in the guidance of my loved ones. Let me be beautiful and serene like the white lotus flower that adorns my wall.

Wrap me in a pink blanket of love
Send prayers and energy at 1 pm

June 5 – 67th Birthday

Yes, I made it to 67 today. This is another milestone for me. Yesterday, I had a big procedure to insert a drain to clear the fluid from the right sac under the lungs. The left lung sac was also drained. Today, and last night, I had tremendous relief. Now, I can feel my other aches and pains—ear, stomach. But they are quite bearable. Tonight I also start a new chemotherapy, VP-16, so there is an adventure ahead. The rainy day will water and nourish my outdoor flowers. Another transition is occurring. Will is going to his MIT Sloan reunion and then back to California, and Alyssa has come back. How comforting to have Michael, Will, and Alyssa with me yesterday. It is now easier to get into bed, so that should facilitate Michael and Alyssa doing it. We will be celebrating today with Sue Lione coming for lunch, and Father Ian coming to say mass. Being present is present enough for me.

I look back on 67 years and reflect on the beautiful words Will and Alyssa shared with me this morning, and it is a life well-lived. There are no regrets—just happiness and gratitude and hope for some more time if that is God's will.

June 5 – Reflections on the end of the day: 67th Birthday

Lavender orchids in a beautiful olive green ceramic pot and a tall rose bush with one beautiful yellow and red rose and the promise of many others were delivered to my door this morning, a gift of Rita Trieger and our yoga kula from Annette Coco's store, Designs by Lee. Beautiful white roses outlined in red were brought in by Maggie Pierce as she came for lunch with Sue Lione. We all enjoyed a lunch of salad, artichoke, avocado, white beans, orange peppers, red onions, kalamata olives topped with seared ahi tuna and chicken breast prepared by Will. Artisan bread with walnuts and Veuve Clicquot champagne completed this luscious birthday lunch, followed by carrot cake for dessert. There was a candle but no lighting because of oxygen in the house. In the afternoon, Father Ian said mass and more flowers arrived.

Pink roses, pink zinnias, and blue nosegays from the Darien High School BC calculus class, gorgeous sunflowers and tall blue flowers from Erin Love. Kitty arrived with her presents of two framed photos, one of us with our daughters, Alyssa and Sarah, and another of us with Michael and Tom. Alyssa gave me beautiful writings this morning and, this evening, a book and icon she purchased in Syria. It was the story of St. Thecla, the first saint circa 100 A.D. There were so many cards that came in the mail from family and friends. A card from last night's book group signed by everyone, a card from Kitty's birthday group signed by everyone. A Fedex arrived from JP and Jen with a new writing journal and cards from Ariana and Liam. Then there were all the phone calls and e-cards—all the family checked in: JP, Jen, Ariana, and Liam, Laird, Sarah, Lisa, Aidan, Chris, Erin, and so many dear friends. Sue Scannell's tilapia dinner and Susan Goodman's dessert treats rounded out a full day, as Alyssa, Michael, and I sat at the table.

I am overwhelmed by all this outpouring of love. I don't know what to say. I think I feel a little sad that I am the recipient and not the giver, that I depend so much on my caregivers. I look back over the last three birthdays and know that I have declined. But I have not given up. My desire to write especially now grows stronger every day. I look forward to writing in the early morning and then at the end of the day. Tonight I also started taking Etoposide, my new friend that will help me get better. I am tolerating the chest tube so much better tonight. Progress is being made on a steady path with incremental little steps—baby steps. I remember Elaine Harris telling me that when I was first diagnosed fourteen years ago: take it one day at a time, little steps, baby steps. It is time for the focus again. I am surrounded by beauty of nature, by the caress and love of family and friends, by faith being ignited by Father Ian, by medical treatments with great promise.

Go away, sadness. Open your heart chakra, open all your chakras to the light.

June 6 – Not Giving Up [2] (with Alyssa)

On Monday, May 18, 2009, I met with my oncologist. He came into the examining room and sat down on a chair across from my husband and me. He had just received the results of a CT scan performed an hour previously. During our fourteen-year journey together he was always positive, always encouraged me. For the past three years, I have had lymphedema in both arms and both legs—a swelling of the limbs caused by poor lymphatic movement as a result of surgery, radiation, and some breast cancer cells in the lymph system. "It is difficult for you, but non-life threatening," he always told me. In January 2009, the edema started accumulating in the abdominal area—adding a tremendous weight gain and making it difficult to bend, move, or even get up from a chair. "We have no remedy for the situation except to try a new chemotherapy which might attack any cancer cells in the lymph system." We did that for a while. Then we stopped the chemotherapy, thinking that giving the body a rest would help more. We always had a future plan of attack, something we would follow with hope.

Now on this Monday, he looked at me with sadness and said, "There is nothing more we can do. There is fluid in the pleural sac under your lungs, making it difficult for you to breathe, and there is fluid around your heart which can cause your heart to collapse." Here was the life-threatening situation.

I then asked a question I never asked before: "How long do I have?"

"It probably won't be tonight, but it could be a week or weeks." I didn't cry, I didn't shout, I accepted what he said without a whimper. But the old fight in me was still there, and I said I wanted to have the fluid drained from around the lungs and heart. He agreed and set up the appointments for the next morning.

Sonograms and x-rays were taken to locate the exact position of the fluid. The cardiologist reported that contrary to the CT scan reading, there was no appreciable fluid around the heart—no imminent danger of the heart collapsing, and my life-threatening situation was removed. The fluid around the lungs was drained, giving immediate breathing relief. Unfortunately, it comes back in several days.

A week later, I had a telephone conference with my naturopath. "You are giving up, and you have never given up." He gave me suggestions of several oral chemotherapies. I now had a fire burning within me— the will to go on knowing it won't be forever but time to still do what I need to do in preparing my final chapter, whenever that may occur.

A consulting oncologist suggested one of the same oral chemotherapies and my oncologist concurred. Hope, faith, peace, and love have filled me. Body, mind, and soul are working together.

I gaze outside at the many hued and varied flowers in my patio against a background of lush greenery set against an azure sky. Birds are singing and chirping all day. I am witness to the renewal of life, nature's gift to me. My spiritual advisor is preparing my soul—God's gift to me.

I am not giving up. I am facing each new day with hope, with a smile on my face, with joy in my heart, which is so filled with love from family and friends. No matter what reality occurs, I am healed.

June 8 – Evening Reflection

So many gifts received today from what I thought would be a routine day. I had my exercise climbing the stairs somewhat under breathing duress. But the visit to Dr. Hall's office and Ann draining the catheter gave great relief as well as feelings of comfort and support from that dear lady who shared her email and phone number with us.

Home, a little rest and lunch delivered by vivacious Debbie Campbell: spinach, artichoke quiche, salad with figs and goat cheese, and pear tart. I basked in the sunlight on the sun porch, ever amazed by the beauty of bluebirds, the sounds of chirping and singing, and the delicate display of multicolored flowers inside and out. My favorite right now is the orchid sent by the yoga group and the rose bush handpicked by Rita Trieger. Jean, the physical therapist, came with new tips and new toys and told Minerva I had enough exercise for the day, so Minerva vacuumed and washed the floor. I had a lovely hour's nap followed by a most welcome visit by Rita, bearing gifts—monk's beads she wears on her arm—the same monks who dedicated a night of prayer to me. Rita dedicated a yoga program she taught in the city to cancer patients in my honor, had the class throw me a birthday party on Tuesday, and she dedicated a chapter she wrote in the *Thread of Yoga* book to me, calling it the "Scarves of the Sisterhood" for the matching scarves that she, Alyssa, and I have from Kripalu.

This woman keeps telling me how much I taught her to be a teacher. I love her for that, but truly I have learned so much from her, and she is so dear to me. She is a pure gift to me.

Lyn Bond came with dinner: quiche, ratatouille, and blondies. Michael, Alyssa, and I had a great dinner, pills taken on time, bed on time, peaceful meditation by Bellaruth Naperstek, and then into bed and final writing.

Blessings flow so unexpectedly. The lotus is glowing brightly on my wall like the white healing light inside my body.

June 9 - Morning Reflection

Darkness at 7 am, but still the flowers on the patio give off a color. Today is Chris' birthday; he is 42 years old. He seems happy. He has and loves Aidan. He and Lisa, Aidan's mother, have a good relationship, and he and Erin are getting along well. He has a job which brings in steady income and is working on his financial problems. Most important, he is sober. I am so proud of him for that.

Michael and Alyssa are up. We are all having breakfast and soon Caroll will be here.

Another day reveals itself.

June 10 – Morning Reflection

It is cloudy again this morning, but there is a promise of light in the sky. Relatively a good night although waking up at 2 am for Tylenol and at 4 am to go to the bathroom. With the help of Corydalis, I went back to bed until 7:30 am, hot water bottle on aching tummy, after having successfully ski-launched into bed. Alyssa has been working on the John Tinker project, and it is ready for proofing. I am so happy she is here with me. My mood is brightening like the clearing blue sky. The birds must be busy at work or visiting, as there are no sounds from them. I heard their wake-up calls at 5:30 am this morning, soothing as balm.

Hello, new day.

June 10 – Evening Reflection

On my birthday, Will wished me peace, love, and hope. They are beautiful virtues. I want to embrace them. Tonight I need perseverance and grace. Perseverance to help breathing, evenly in and out until it becomes smoother. The grace to do this without a lot of flailing and attention. It is so hard, and I know how supportive Michael and Alyssa are with me tonight. So let me take myself on a journey, a Bernie Siegel journey to a castle where there is a strong box filled with all the tools I need to ride this out. I know it still may be uncomfortable, but it will be better after tomorrow, and our plan after that will help me ride this out.

Take me deep into dream land to walk in fields of flowers in the sunlight, to sit on a daisy flower, to feel the touch of butterflies and the kiss of the dew. Lord, I pray for your grace and perseverance this night.

June 11 – Evening Reflection (with Alyssa)

Such a difference between breathing last night and tonight. We know how to drain and avoid the crisis and see how it works with just one lung for now. There are other worries for Michael and Alyssa that I had not been cognizant of, namely, blisters on legs that have opened and are draining lymph fluid. I know that I must now really prioritize, work on collating my writings, any letters, and work on my final chapter. I am seeing Father Ian on Friday for general confession. Peter Cullen says that I am fine as I am. God is holding my hand.

I am being myself with my friends—honest and accepting—and they are loving towards me. I guess those who do not know what to say or do are staying away. Alyssa is here for two more nights, and then she will go back to California for a week to ten days. I know she has to go, and I want her to do it, but I will miss her so terribly much. I just found out that JP is coming on Monday. That is something to look forward to. We will write and share.

Chris and Will call in every day, and I know they have plans to come back too. All my handicapped accessories, my new clothes, and my lift chair have helped very much. I also now have a sturdy table for the draining supplies.

I am not fighting about getting into bed too early. It feels good.

I am so happy Alyssa suggested writing tonight. I think I might like to hear a Bernie Siegel meditation before going to sleep. My body is rooting for the new chemotherapy. If it is God's will, it will help me.

I want to erase the worry from my husband. I am in distress when I cannot breathe. Sometimes my ear hurts. Otherwise I've gotten used to my situation. I am grateful for all my caregivers. I am humbled. I am still smiling. I am still happy and hopeful. I am a flower—a pink flower, a rose, opening up its petals to the world.

June 12 – Morning Reflection: Things You Have Lost

Pretty good night of sleep. I could tell that the Vicodin had worn off when I awoke at 2 am. Michael gave me two Corydalis, and I dozed on and off until 5:30 am. Bad stomach ache this morning that accelerated while at the kitchen table. I took Gaviscon and Miralax, hoping it would abate. It became severe enough that I threw up, but it is now abating with aid of hot water bottle. I wish I could figure out what causes this upset.

This morning the imagery Bobbie Earle sent in her email entered my mind of the vase at Drew Lamm's house on Thursday with all the tulips limp and bent over, and one solitary tulip standing up straight. After laughing so hard, they generated the prompt: "Things you have lost."

I think of myself as the lone solitary tulip standing up straight. I could and have written on what I have lost, figuratively and literally. But the survivor tulip speaks to me this morning. I picture it white, in the middle of the vase, standing proud, and not upset by the loss of all the tulips around it. The standing tulip is seeking the sunlight, breathing the air, absorbing the beauty of the room, listening to sound vibrations, standing, savoring, thriving.

What experiences will I feel today? I know I have draining, Reiki, and confession on the schedule and perhaps some phone calls. I will remember that I am that solitary tulip, strong and tall, looking out with anticipation to this new day. I have Alyssa here with me—her last full day for a while. I will treasure every moment.

June 12 – Evening Reflection (with Alyssa)

It was a good day, starting with a shower and the welcome draining of 600 cc from the pleural cavity. Amazing how fast it fills. Michael performed a very good job, considering he had an audience of four. The procedures were time consuming. I came downstairs and had breakfast in the family room—bran yogurt with fruit—and Caroll, Alyssa, and I all had coffee with banana bread. Katherine Silvan came at 11:30 am to do Reiki in her sweet, quiet manner, promising to be back again on Tuesday. Terry Scarborough, a very dear friend, brought a delicious lunch, which we ate in the family room: lentil soup with spinach and sweet potato, watermelon salad with feta and olives, and green salad with blueberries. I moved to the porch and sat in my new lift chair, so easy to get in and out of, and started Art Jones's book, *Facing Fear with Faith*. It contains some beautiful poetry. Minerva came at 3 pm; we walked and stretched, and Father Ian came at 4:30, and I had a general confession. It was conversational, covering the sins of my life, some of which I may have confessed before. I can tell him anything. We talked for a long time, and then he absolved my sins and gave me my penance (saying the Lenten prayer) and the blessing followed by communion.

Stiff from sitting until 6 pm and cold from the AC, I walked into the kitchen as the McBrearitys were bringing dinner: two filet mignons, spinach, rice, fruit, salad, and chocolate chip cookies. They are such dear friends. I tried to eat wisely and sparingly, savoring every delicious morsel and particularly enjoying fruit, frozen chocolate yogurt, and a chocolate chip cookie. We returned to the family room for a few minutes and Skyped with Will who played golf at 6:30 am, worked all day, and is going to the Giants game tonight. Ah, youth — how I remember those days packed with so many diverse experiences. Do it while you're young and while you can. I took my Ativan and Corydalis and VP-16 and am in bed at 9:30 pm.

My soul is purified, I am at peace. I am ready to accept what may come next. I still feel nervous about going from this life to the next. It is the unknown. Every human being faces that crossing over. I have much to prepare for that. I look forward to creating a legacy of words and love.

June 13 – Morning Reflection

Birds are happily chirping as the rain has stopped, the sky is clearing, and the flowers are perking up. I look forward to this morning, draining the fluid, getting dressed, and painting with Georgia Young.

Vince and Tina arrive around noon, about the same time that Alyssa leaves for California, with Joe Taicner taking her to the airport.

I look forward to a day of reflection, of reading, resting, visiting, of marshalling my resources. I am at peace with the world and with myself. Concentrate on my writing for my priorities, my family. I follow that thread as my focus, a silken thread to pull me along, thin but strong as a thread from a silkworm before weaving a beautiful scarf.

June 14 – Evening Reflection

Today was a new adventure in the shower, sitting on a white plastic shower seat with Pansy, the weekend day nurse, also in the shower, shoes off but socks on. We used the hand shower only and, amazingly, the only thing that got wet on her were her socks. The shower seat felt secure, and we still had to work out the mechanics of the grab bars.

Vince and Tina's visit was lovely, although quite short. Tina teared up at JP's and Will's toasts on the wedding video. Joanne and Bill Santulli brought communion. Vince and Tina left at noon, and I took a nice nap. I awoke and sat on the porch, and visiting nurse Marita arrived. I did manage the treadmill for ten minutes, with breaks in between.

Mary Lee MacDougall came for a short visit. It is always such a pleasure to be in her presence. She is so positive and such an affirmation for me. When she left, Marita prepared me for bed (at 5 pm), and then we ate dinner. So at 6:30 pm, we are completely ready, and I have time to read, write, and reflect.

As I look outside the kitchen window and reflect tonight, I see the flowers struggling to perk up after days of rain. I feel like the flowers, struggling to perk up. Am I missing Alyssa? Of course I am. But JP will be here soon, and then Chris, and Michael is by my side. I am blessed.

Father Ian says my soul is being purified, and I am becoming a saint. All I know is that I have accepted my dependence and humbleness and feel free, at one with love and beauty, friends, and family. I feel open like a vessel being emptied. I know what sustains me is love, the love of my husband, children, grandchildren, and friends.

The next step in my transformation is concentrating on God's love for me. I am working on that plunge. It is intangible as if putting your arms around a cloud or holding a sunbeam in your hand. Dusk comes, the birds chirp goodnight, and my lotus flower awaits me overlooking my bed.

June 15 – Evening

This is the opening of the art hanging at the New Canaan YMCA. I wish I could attend these events, but that is not possible at this time. The site of my catheter hurts today. Michael said it does not look red. Luckily I see Dr. Hall tomorrow. It makes me ponder what direction to go with the left side. It is good that there are still decisions I can make for myself, as hard as they may be.

Have I not turned everything over to God? God doesn't say to give up, just to trust and have faith, hope, and love.

It is my faith to believe that I am important to God, just as He mentions the lilies in the field. I am a micro speck in God's big creation. Look at a blade of grass as it trembles with life, making chlorophyll to stay green, housing worms, ants, beetles, soil microorganisms. Go down within the green, the soothing color. Add a dash of yellow and it turns blue, add a dash of red and it turns purple. So our lives turn, so easily.

June 16 – Evening Reflection (with JP)

I feel happy tonight—a different feeling from hopeful—happy is happy. JP is here for one. I am breathing better for two. So today is good. The meatloaf and mashed potatoes bring back memories of happiness of early married days. We were frugal, thrifty, and happy with a baby on our hip.

The sunlight bathed the patio as we returned from Dr. Hall's visit and draining and Bennett CBC and chest x-ray, offering us lunch outside in its embracing light. My appetite returns when I can breathe. I feel that I can swallow and digest. But don't be misled. There is not all that much room there.

I am looking at this one solitary rose in a vase left over from the dozen Maggie Pierce brought for my birthday—white with pink edges. Some of the bottom edges of the petals are frayed and tattered, but the flower is still elegant. It is a sign to me of how I can continue, strong and tall, courageous and positive. So many decisions have yet to be made, but I go day by day, keeping pace with one baby step after baby step, and thankful for that gait. The vagaries of each day swing like a person on a trapeze. The constants are my routine with my caregivers, my day to day ablutions, visitors, lunches and dinners, family visitors, and of course, my writing—sometimes just recording the day, sometimes taking me to uncharted territory.

Oh, let me wander in my dreams through wildflower fields or float on a cloud looking down on verdant pastures. Let me think of God and how one day I will join His perfect spirit.

June 17 – Being Ready (with JP)

I am ready for many things. I am ready for positive emotions, being joyful, hopeful, and happy, being in the moment, admiring flowers, painting flowers, writing about my feelings, seeing my family and friends, sitting in the sunshine, reading a good book, watching my TV shows.

I am not ready yet to face mortality and death, although I know it exists and will come as it comes eventually to everyone. I have not quite found the absolute answer yet from Father Ian, although I appreciate all the ground we have covered. I am hoping that Peter Cullen and Bill Scheyd may give some further elucidation. But deep down, I know the true analysis must come from me.

At the moment of death, the soul leaves the body, carrying with it intellect and free will. My soul will either go to Purgatory for purification and suffer the pain of not being with God, or it will join God in heaven. At the moment of death, we will see before us all our sins of commission and omission. Once we are purified, we will join God in heaven, although I have no idea what that will be like.

At the same time, while I think of the next life, I have a strong role in this life, and I am ready for any changes, medical and personal, that may occur, especially good changes. I pray for good changes. My pen guides me along this smooth lined paper, down winding roads, past crooked trees, in clearings of flowers and brooks rushing over strong outcroppings in the water. My memory recalls the great gorge of Cornell and the sad events that took place as well as the jubilant ones. Take me down to a bower where willows and palm trees are intertwined, and leave me in comfort to reflect.

June 18 – One Month

Jean-Paul reminded me that today is one month since our meeting with Bar. I am breathing better and that is good progress. Michael is doing a super job draining the fluid from the lung. But the fluid in the rest of the body has not abated, so I am still very dependent. Exercising the legs and arms helps with mobility.

Having Jean-Paul here has been a wonderful gift. I treasure every moment I am with him, and will miss him when he returns, but return to his family he must. I hope he will come again. How special it is that we are writing and sharing.

My writings are a chronology and history of these past weeks. I don't know what is going to happen, but I am peaceful and open. I still want more time with my family and to accomplish my list of priorities written in the back of this journal. My spiritual advisors are each a little different. Father Ian insists my soul needs to be purified so that I can be with God, and that such a process is happening now. Peter Cullen says God is holding my hand. He himself believes in life everlasting, but he personally has not considered the passage from life to the next. Bill Scheyd says God is loving and merciful and just to have faith and not worry about anything. What do I think? I know that I have not yet said I am ready to go, Lord. I guess I want to keep hanging on for a while. I am like that rose in my vase, lasting, upright, smiling. Even the rain does not bother me. There is so much beauty inside with all the flowers and love from family and friends. These are my blessings. Although sometimes I am incredulous that all this happened so fast, I know that I am blessed, that my husband and children can prepare with me to say goodbye. One wish is that they will all be with me at that time, holding my hands and looking into my eyes.

Tonight I will try to be a musical song, light and sweet, lulling me to dreamland and healing as sleep will do for me.

June 19 – Breaking the Rules (with Chris)

From a young child through my adulthood, I always adhered to the rules. My sense of what was expected of me, being polite, working hard, and to the best of my ability, obeying the rules of the road and the rules of the Catholic faith, with some exceptions. It worked well for me, gave me structure and a guide. I have now reached the point in my life when I feel there are no rules per se—no rules to break and no rules to make, just living as best as I can each day, working hard to make it a good day and grateful for each new day and the people who come to share their love with food and good wishes and especially my children and husband. I am so blessed with my family.

If I could design a day, it would be without the feeling of being tied to the earth, dependent on help to get up from a chair, shower, dress. I would like to be a butterfly or hummingbird or even a waft of air free floating, light and airy—free, not worried about falling but letting myself truly embrace this new feeling. Perhaps that is what it is like to pass from life to death and live in the afterlife. I'll have to let you know all about it.

June 23 – Tuesday

Chris left yesterday, and Alyssa arrived. I am happy to have her here, and I know that Michael is too. Going to bed later (11 pm rather than 9:30 or 10) enabled me to stay in bed until 5:45 am. I was waiting to hear the birds as my wake-up signal but never did. They were silent this morning. The light filtering in the room told me it was morning.

As I sit at the kitchen table looking out, I see the flowers in a semi-circle in front of me as if I am on a stage. Their little heads of color are opening up after so many days of rain. The herbs—parsley, basil, oregano, and rosemary—are thriving.

I am avoiding the stomach ache, so that is thriving. I am ready to be drained again this morning.

Today is my appointment with Dr. Thau to have the left lung tapped. It does make me nervous because of potential complications, but the rewards will be worth it. I have decided for now not to have a drain placed on the left. I believe that I can tolerate the left lung with fluid as long as the right lung cavity is drained twice a day.

It is a new day this Tuesday, to be filled with the visit to Dr. Thau, the Beinsteins' visit here, then talking, sharing, relaxing with Alyssa, reading, writing, working on my writings 2009 book project, and setting up an appointment for the writing group to come here.

Caregivers will arrive and go, Pansy today instead of Caroll, then Minerva. Perhaps today with lungs emptied, I can walk on the treadmill.

A new day unfolds.

June 23 – Afternoon Reflection

I am on a Vicodin high right now. All pain is dulled. This morning's tap with Dr. Thau went well, but it was still a challenge. We all agreed that it is not a good idea to tap again. Which means a drain on the left side eventually. Alyssa and I both shared our morning reflections with each other, as we had time before the procedure started. I was absolutely blown away by the sharing of her deep feelings. I love her so very much and want to understand her more fully. I thought she didn't want children, but perhaps she does and can't have them for some reason. Her age of 40 is on the outer limits, but still a possibility. So many women are becoming pregnant for the first time in their 40's. I know of no one who would be a better mother. The desire for motherhood is amazing. Kim Fisher, whom I never thought would want children, as she openly stated that, is now expecting her second child at age 42.

If Alyssa did become pregnant, would God give me the strength and perseverance to survive and see and hold this baby? There could be no stronger motivation, even stronger than the desire to write with her at Lake Tahoe.

But I want her to know that whatever happens, I will accept. It is just so wonderful to understand her so deeply. I believe that in this visit, we will explore deeply, openly, honest, full of love, as always.

June 23 – Evening Reflection (with Alyssa)

I feel energetic tonight. Being able to breathe with both lungs is something I never took for granted, but appreciated like warm sunlight on a soft gentle breeze. Deep yoga breaths and Tai Chi breathing—in and out—told me, "Be grateful you can breathe easily." How significant that I appreciated that so much. I now realize that it is not just the shortness of breath, but also the sapping of energy and the slow movements that result from breathing difficulties. Luckily, we have found the formula of draining twice a day. It is also strong evidence to have a catheter placed in the left side when I feel ready for another OR procedure.

For tonight, I will revel in the moment, listening to music, sharing with my darling Alyssa. These are my blessings for today, including Michael's capable draining completing the picture. Even though we bicker as Alyssa says, I do love and appreciate him very much. I will listen to a meditation before sleep and pray for a long, healing sleep tonight.

I have been opened like the white lotus flower on my wall, offering up its great beauty, peaceful and contemplative but aware of the vibrations of love and blessing.

June 24 – Afternoon Reflection (with Alyssa)

After a long sleep last night, up at 4 am for bathroom then back to bed until 7:30 am, I feel refreshed and energetic this morning. My patience, compassion, and loving nature have been rejuvenated. We drained this morning, then breakfast, then Pansy helped with a shower, and I was downstairs in time for Father Ian at 10:30 am.

Ian talked about Sunday's Gospel when the apostles were in a boat with Jesus on the Sea of Galilee and a sudden storm blew up. They kept bailing water out of the boat. Nevertheless, the water kept deluging in. They were very afraid and woke Jesus and said, "Do you not care if we perish?"

Jesus stood up and calmed the waters and said, "Do you not trust that I will take care of you? I am here with you." Jesus, likewise, is always with us even when we are suffering. He is with us. Ian then segued into being kind and compassionate with others. My cue to stop bickering with Michael. Be patient, understanding, and kind.

Mary Runestad came for lunch, bearing egg salad sandwiches, turkey sandwiches, chips, fruit, and chocolate chip cookies. Sharon Bray called for a chat. It is so nice of her to keep thinking of me. I saw a picture of Sharon, her daughter, and her four-month old grandson. He is a beautiful baby.

That brings me to the wonderful discussion Alyssa and I had this morning when she shared her deep and personal thoughts with me. I was so touched. She and Laird would welcome a baby if they became pregnant. It makes me so happy to know they feel this way. It will be so wonderful for them if it happens. I will pray for them every day. Dear Lord, if it is your will, please let it happen. I am motivated to not give up but to keep going and do whatever I can and whatever I must do to be here for them. Please God, with your strength and grace, I can do this.

It will mean another drain. It will also mean attention to the ear, which has become painful and now has two swollen bumps, which were not there before. I am sure that Bar will not allow me to have surgery to remove them, so it will mean radiation to the ear, which means stopping the chemo for a month—two weeks beforehand and during the two weeks of radiation, and perhaps a week or two afterwards. But I'll make that decision down the road. Meanwhile, I will continue to enjoy the day and wear the oxygen meter on my finger tonight.

Thank you, God, for my daughter, Alyssa. She is one of the biggest blessings in my life.

June 25 – Thursday Morning Reflection

Successful treatment of the overnight oxygen test. Up at 3 am for bathroom, then back to bed; up at 6:15 am this morning. Breakfast early. Alyssa is awake and with us. Caroll arrives, sponge bath, dress, Miltex, and rest. Ear very painful, dulled a bit by Tylenol.

I see Alyssa writing, sitting across from me in the green chair in the family room. How wonderful is that. She is so beautiful inside and out. I see the lavender orchid plants and the white lilies on the piano across from me. I see red and pink roses on the round glass table to my right. I am surrounded by beauty. The sun is shining in the bay window. We go out to see Dr. Hall today. I am glad it has stopped raining for now. I would love to feel some sun on my face and on my ear. If it is not too humid, perhaps I can sit outside in the sun for ten minutes.

Jean Meyer worked on my legs for almost an hour yesterday. It definitely increased flexibility, and I could tell I was more movable in bed and could get in and out of bed easier.

I closed my eyes for a moment and found myself dozing off, dreaming of a milkshake. What a childhood memory—sitting at the counter of the drug store in Bayonne, New Jersey, on a high stool, white and grey marble top, stool with wire back in shape of two fans side by side. I watch the shake being prepared, whirring in the metal blender. Then the metal cup comes off. It is ready and poured into a tall glass for me, served with a big straw and a long spoon. The metal cup is placed next to the glass for me to have a refill or share with someone. Sometimes my mother or father is there with me, and I share it with them. I may have to treat everyone to a Baskin-Robbins shake today. I will have mine made with frozen yogurt, preferably vanilla. Michael will have strawberry. And Alyssa, I am not sure which flavor she will choose. Pretty soon we will exercise, then lunch, coffee, and off to see Dr. Hall and Ann and draining. Just one bottle today, thank you. I will submit my poem that I wrote in Sharon Bray's class on May 6 for her to post on her website, writingthroughcancer.com.

I will write some more on my final chapter and give some attention to my 2009 book project. It sounds like a good, productive day. Tonight, Alyssa and I will watch a chick flick on DVD. I want to do as much as I can with her by my side. I love her so much.

June 26 – A Recent Walk or Journey and What I Have Seen

My recent journey was to the doctor yesterday and then to town for a vanilla milkshake. What did I see in a new way? I saw the charm of the town of New Canaan. People walking purposely or just wandering from store to store. I saw women wearing different outfits—more revealing than would ever have been acceptable years ago. However, they were beautiful, thin women, showing off their beauty, as an artist would render a painting. There was a woman in her 30's with slim black pants and a lavender top lined in black material—thin and clinging—molding her breasts, nipples perky. A young woman in her twenties was wearing a navy suit and clinging sleeves, a scooped white top with a black belt pulling her outfit together.

We parked in front of what formerly was Villarina, now Patio.com, where Alyssa bought the wonderful table that serves as a holder for the draining equipment. The lamp store is now a store selling bathing suits—upscale. Stores come and go. It was nice to be out going for a ride. Once home, I walked to the patio and sat in the green reclining chair in the sun, hat and sunglasses on in the midst of the flowers on the patio all perking up in the sun. How glorious. Closed eyes and took a nap.

The blood chemistry fax arrived—electrolytes low—especially the potassium—near danger point, I thought. Have to deal with that soon—mobilize resources. Also, one side of mouth swollen— another concern. But today, I have let it go a little—put it in God's hands.

June 27 – Morning Reflection (with Alyssa)

Having just finished breakfast, sitting at the table looking out, I see the sunlight filtering between the green leaves of the trees, the remnants of rain on the leaves sparkling like diamonds. The dew on the sunlit patches of grass are likewise shining, little white twinkle lights deep in the blades. The flowers, having received plenty of watering, are straight and open, waiting for the promise of the warm sun once the rays move over the patio. I am shedding grogginess and worry and ill humor and embracing the beauty of nature. It is a reminder not to fixate on the little things that disturb as someone amenable can be found to take care of them. And to turn over the big issues and concerns and health issues that I can't control to God's hands, praying for God's grace, strength, and direction for me and my doctors.

Finally, I must keep foremost in my mind to direct my attention to my caregivers first and me second, always thanking them and showing my appreciation, being compassionate, and patient. The love bestowed is returned one-hundred fold.

June 28 – Afternoon Reflection, Sunday

I just finished reading Kelly Corrigan's *The Middle Place,* and actually I
am a bit jealous that she is cancer-free after a lumpectomy, chemo and
radiation, and that her 75-year-old dad continues to beat cancer—
prostate and bladder. Ok, that said, let me look at my blessings and
my extreme gratitude for this beautiful day spent with Alyssa sitting
on the enclosed porch, sharing, reading, having lunch, getting up and
stretching and walking, seeing the baby robins in their nest just outside
the dining room in the bush. We capped off the day by toasting each
other with Veuve Clicquot brought over to us by our friend Gina.

Father Ian came with communion this afternoon and read his readings
for the day, discussed the gospel and shared the essence of his homily.
His daytime prayer was based on 1 John "God is love," which was the
theme for our Emmaus XVI. He again reiterated to have faith and trust
in God, for God is with us always, even when we think He's not. He
said to me, "You must live in the moment," and I told him that is
exactly what I do. I don't even know the schedule for the next day. I
am living in the moment. That is my life now and will continue. But I
am looking forward to a delicious dinner and perhaps a chick flick
with Alyssa, time permitting. Before I know it, bedtime will arrive, and
this glorious day will come to a close.

June 30 – Morning Reflection

This morning I received an email from Will saying, "Rejoice in this day
the Lord has made. Enjoy the day, Mom." How wonderful is that, and
it sets the tone for my day. After a restful night's sleep, we did our
morning ritual—draining, breakfast, upstairs for shower. Today, this
morning, I started the Prednisone to treat the drooping left side of my
face. I am wearing my sexy new black skirt purchased by Alyssa. I
would love to wear it with just my slides, but Michael feels they are
irritating my toe. We discussed buying another pair with open toes for
the warm weather. Perhaps a car trip to Hawley Lane Shoes on
Wednesday?

I am writing, sitting on the porch looking out at the greenery, the
sunlight warming the tops of the trees and highlighting the leaves in
light green against the darker green background. The day ahead will

be fun. Georgia Young is coming to paint with me this morning. Then Holley for lunch, Katherine for Reiki, Jean for exercise (with Minerva), then Maggie and Harrison bringing dinner. Judy Boughrum may also drop in with Jeff. I will get ready early for bed, knowing that I will be tired after such a full day and look forward to finishing the movie *Nights in Rodante* with Alyssa. She and I will celebrate this beautiful day together, today, the last day of June.

July 1 – What Wisdom do you Have to Share Today (with Alyssa)

Accept what is the reality of the moment and blossom with it. When we moved back to France in 1982, I attended an orientation workshop at the American Church in Paris called, "Bloom Where You Are Planted." That is the wisdom. Even with a bad stomach ache, I can ride it out and figure out what I need to do to make it better. Number one is rest, and I am so happy for this quiet, relaxing day. As I sit on the porch in my lift chair, I am looking at the beautiful purple orchids in front of me, lifting their heads to the sun, so happy to be in here, as I am. My new prayer shawl is a beautiful purple like the orchids and was crocheted by a woman in St. John's parish and delivered to Darien High School for Michael to bring home to me. It is beautiful handiwork and crocheted in the shape of a "V." The students at Darien High School have been a loving and supportive community, impressing me with their generosity and kindness to me and Michael, sending flowers, raising money for the Bennett Cancer Center, and sending many cards with personal messages to Michael expressing their care and appreciation for him.

Number two on riding out the stomach ache is determining what food would make it feel better this morning. Miso soup and toast and Gaviscon were the right decision. Also analyze what may have caused the problem and don't repeat that. Spicy soup for lunch, spicy shrimp for dinner; overall, a lot of food eaten, my meds including Prednisone, and a very busy day were all contributors. Today, I am in control of a very bland diet and quiet day.

One concern I have had that is out of my control is spending ten hours a day with a caregiver, day in and day out, while Michael is teaching.

He just said that Caroll may do it, which would be good since I know her, and she knows my routine. Would she be able to take me to doctors' visits and out for a ride once in a while? I know it will be a period of adjustment, of planning each day, which I can control.

My wisdom as I reflect on this is to take it one day at a time, and enjoy that day fully rather than looking at it as a long, dull period of time. Time is a jewel to cherish, polish, and wear happily and gratefully. I can read, I can write, exercise, watch my programs, have breakfast, bathe, have lunch, nap, and the day will pass quickly. A friend may visit now and then, and I'll speak with my children every day. It sounds like a good plan.

Alyssa mentioned working on the "Book of J" and writing my wisdom for the next generation. I like that. I also want to expand "The Quilt of My Life," which may be included in the "Book of J."

I like what Alyssa reminded me that I told her when she was getting married: never go to bed angry, always look nice for your husband, and do something for yourself so you bring something exciting into the marriage. I will include that wisdom in the "Book of J."

July 2 – Afternoon Check-In (with Alyssa)

It has been a busy day, going to see Dr. Hall with Ann draining (I gave her the *Vicky Cristina Barcelona* movie), CBC at the Bennett Center, Donna T made decaf coffee for me, then off to Hawley Lane shoes to find open toe shoes (no success but Alyssa and Michael found and ordered a pair on the Internet), then to Fabulous Feasts for a quesadilla and wrap for lunch.

We just had time for lunch, and Deb Pantalina arrived to do reflexology. She wanted to do facial reflexology, but she could not read my face from the back of the chair. Next time she comes in three weeks, I can give her the black step stool. Father Ian was just here with communion and his daily offering, reading from The Book of Amos. He is going on vacation tomorrow to be with his family on Long Island and will not be back until July 10 and then work on the Adult Emmaus weekend, so it will be a while until I see him again. It will be time for Msgr. Bill Scheyd.

How do I feel today? I had a wonderful, supportive thought for the day from Will, saying my gifts of myself have touched my friends who come and visit and show their love for me now. I had such a good pain-free sleep, and that fact plus the Prednisone has me energized. Actually, the Prednisone has me hyper. I look forward to sharing Veuve Clicquot tonight with Alyssa, Laird, and Michael. I will go easy on the eating at dinner.

It was good to be outside, riding in the car, going to Bennett and seeing people. My new lavender prayer shawl was the perfect wrap for today's outing.

Yesterday was such a super day with Alyssa and watching a movie at night. Today also we are spending time together—so precious to me, my darling daughter whom I love so much.

July 3 – Every Week is a Fresh Start (with Will)

Today marks a new set of visitors, as Will and Sarah arrived this morning. Tomorrow as Will and Sarah participate in July 4th activities, Alyssa and Laird will spend the day here, and then they leave on Sunday to return to California. Will and Sarah are delightful to be with, and I am so happy that they are here.

I believe this week will be challenging but good. We will write every day and talk and share. We will get some projects accomplished, writings typed, photos organized, Alaska book completed. I will look forward to enjoying every day, living in the moment, appreciating the flowers, nature, and warmth and caring of family and friends.

On the medical side, we will have to deal with the ear. Hopefully Bar will agree to radiation while I am still on the VP-16, and the radiation in turn will curb some of the tumor growth. The chest is holding but not cleared as it once was, and new bumps appear now and then.

Today is a more tired day and then a more down day for no apparent reason, and I find that bothersome. My back pain has eased off, and my ear is very annoying, and my jaw pains, but I can breathe. So this week, I want to blossom like the lilies on my piano, open buds closed to pain and sadness, open up to the air and the sun, smile, and take in the wonderful life that hums in my body and all around me. I hope I can sit a while in the sunshine, warmed by the rays lingering on my face and neck.

July 3 – Evening Reflection (with Will)

Today started out tired and slow, but I did revive over the hours. I so much enjoyed spending the day with Will and Sarah, and we had a delicious dinner together of pasta with beets, beet greens, and Chevre cheese.

I am ready for bed at 9 pm, and Will and Sarah seem to be ready for bed too. My breathing is a little labored tonight even after draining. I wonder if it can be the accumulation in the left lung. My chest has opened up some. I will not worry about these things, but keep taking relaxing breaths, visualization and meditation, and it may be time for a Belleruth Naperstek meditation tonight. Can I convince Will to put some flower essence on my feet once I am in bed? I am happy for a deep, peaceful sleep tonight, free from pains and strange dreams. I will embrace the healing powers of sleep and rest. The Prednisone will be over in two days, and the face has improved.

I glance once more at the white lilies open to the air and to life, and I remind myself to do the same.

July 4 – Long-lasting (with Alyssa)

Long-lasting and everlasting apply to so many emotions, feelings, and behaviors, but not to health and life. Hopefully health and life are long-lasting, never everlasting. For everlasting, the life and health of the soul or spirit is the rule, and that is a part of who we are during our lives. It is a comfort that this means we can be everlasting.

Happily, many things are long-lasting during our lives. Love, friendship, happiness, and family can all be examples of long-lasting. I have been blessed with all of these. I am truly blessed and so thankful. My health was excellent until I was 52, but even with the diagnosis of breast cancer, I could function very well including seven years cancer-free, and continuing my career as an attorney with recurrences. Only in the past nine months have the challenges become steeper, more acute. The past two months have been a turning point towards less mobility and nearly complete dependence on caregivers, a very humbling experience; the fact of my mortality is more evident. No one ever knows from day to day, but my situation gives me time to prepare myself, write my legacy, and spend so much quality time with Michael and my children. I thank God for them every day. They are beyond supportive. They are pure unconditional love, and I love them back the same way. It's not that I am giving up. I am always hopeful, doing what I can to survive and thrive. At the same time, I am realistic. I know I should not worry but place my faith and trust in God's hands.

These past two weeks with Alyssa have been so wonderful. What a treasured 4th of July today with Alyssa and Laird, Will and Sarah, and Michael and I all sharing a beautiful meal at lunch and then a wonderful dinner prepared by Michael and shared with Alyssa and Laird, Michael's specialty: salmon over bok choy and mashed sweet potato, swiss chard with garlic snapes. Tonight I am ready for bed early, have been wrapped, and once it is dark we will watch the fireworks in New York harbor.

My family, my children are long-lasting. To me, they are everlasting because they will continue to carry me in their hearts and memory.

July 5 – Sunday Reflection (with Alyssa, Will, and Pansy)

A good night's sleep and a nice breakfast after draining and upstairs sponge bath started off this glorious day of cool, dry weather, for now at least. Alyssa, Laird, Michael, Will, and I all had breakfast together. The Crosses stopped in with Carolyn on their way with Sarah to PJ's Kitchen for breakfast. Now we are sitting and writing together on the sun porch. How special this is.

Today marks a transition, as Alyssa and Laird return to California. I will miss them both, with all our conversations, meals together, and sharing time together. I will especially miss Alyssa: all her caring, loving ways and all the activities we have engaged in together. I know she'll be back soon. In the meantime, Will and Sarah are here, and Will has ably resumed charge of the schedule and to some extent of me. I look forward to our special time together.

From my chair, I can see the shadows from the leaves and trees moving gently side to side on the white singles at the back of the house on the patio. It reminds me of a plant attached to a rock in a gentle current of water, undulating as the water flows over the rock and combs out its tendrils then curls it again. And likewise, I am moved along gently while looking at the sun painting some trees and leaves the lightest green, by my family and Pansy and the love in this room, nurturing and caressing.

This is the day the Lord has made. Let us give thanks and be glad.

July 5 – Sunday Evening Reflection (with Will and Sarah)

Today, I discussed my current situation with both Will and Sarah. I was impressed to hear their words that I am adjusting, seem better, and the view is more optimistic. I share these sentiments to a great extent, knowing that we have come a long way since we met with Michael Bar on May 18, with his prognosis of only a few weeks left. The immobilization and dependency are ever present. Certain things have aided the coping comfortably with what is the reality now: the hospital bed, the lift chair, the walker, the grab bars in the bathroom shower, the raised toilet with its grab bars, and the half step. As a child learns to walk for the first time, I too took first steps in my humbleness and dependence to fashion a routine. My morning caregivers aid me with shower and personal hygiene. My afternoon caregiver guides my leg exercises, so essential to staying limber and free from cramping. We have learned so much — what to eat to maintain sufficient sodium and electrolyte balance, when to eat it, how much to eat. Michael and I have figured a way to enter the hospital bed quickly and efficiently, which can again be utilized if I must get up to go to the bathroom during the night.

I have learned that I must let some things go. I miss my bed and sharing it with Michael upstairs in the Zen space of my bedroom. I am accepting the hospital bed as a necessity. So many changes in such a short amount of time. We had to work through all of them. It was not easy, but I realize it is the right thing to do. There are still many challenges, the ear being one big decision-making event.

Tempering these coping skills, we are developing medical procedures that we follow every day, such as draining for easier breathing, and times of Reiki, reflexology, visiting, and spiritual direction.

Overall, I have my writing projects, which are my central core, along with my watercolor painting and to-do lists of completion of cataloguing oil paintings annotated by stories of the prominence of each one.

I am evolving like Darwin's species, guided by the light and fire within me rather than by random chance.

I reflect now that it may be time for bed and healing sleep.

July 6 – Preparation for New Treatment (with Will)

Today was such a beautiful day. We sat on the porch comfortably, the sun shining. We wrote then worked on the description of paintings project. I closed my eyes for a little rest. Kathy Pasternak and Paula Ryan visited and brought lunch. Gina Barber brought communion. I read then moved to the family room and exercised with Minerva. Rita Trieger came for a visit, and Penny Cattrell when she brought dinner.

Frank Messino answered Michael's call of this morning, leaving message that I was ready to start radiation at his convenience. He scheduled measurement and a first treatment for tomorrow, at 3 pm, first cautioning that I must stop the VP-16 during the period of radiation. The chemo can be synergistic with the radiation, causing additional skin burning.

I am ready for the treatment, having done sufficient investigation into an alternative method, PTP, in South Carolina, and having given sufficient time, one month, to determine if the VP-16 might change the outlook of the ear. That has not happened, and the scabs continue to accumulate and move down under the ear. The pain comes more often in the ear and jaw area. The cranial nerve has been compressed, causing a Bell's-like palsy on the left side of the face. Frank said he would go to plan B on the radiation, namely, less intense and allowing my back and head to be elevated rather than lying flat. He is not having a CT scan done, so that I do not have to lie flat for that. I wish I would have a CT scan, but he seems confident with the anatomy. I will discuss it with him. Also, I will ask him if the lesser radiation will allow re-radiation if needed. I feel comfortable that this must be done. I will go peacefully, aided by half an Ativan and with a later draining to facilitate breathing.

Tomorrow, a new treatment, a new adventure, which I am accepting as my help, my friend. Attitude is everything.

July 8 – Changes

I had my second radiation today, and already my ear is changing. The scabs are falling off, thanks to the radiation and application of Aquaphor which softens them. That is very welcome.

Another change is my better breathing because of draining twice a day and along with that some weight loss and renewed energy. That is very welcome.

Chris and Aidan arrived tonight, and I am so happy to have them here. That is very welcome.

Will and Sarah return tomorrow to California after a wonderful week together. I am so happy that they came to spend the time with me. Their return is not welcome, but I know it is necessary, so I say goodbye for now with a happy and grateful heart, a heart full of love.

Michael and I have modified our routines; they have changed and work better. Getting into bed is easier, doing what needs to be done every day, getting ready for bed, are all easier. These are welcome changes.

The fire and determination within me has grown stronger. That is a welcome change.

I am doing better in a way than I was a few weeks ago. That is a welcome change.

My desire to write has increased; my appreciation of each day has intensified; my faith is stronger. These are welcome changes.

Life evolves around positive changes.

July 11 – The Middle Place: How I Was Then, How I am Now (with Chris)

To reflect on how I was before my cancer diagnosis, I have to go back to 1995 or earlier. I remember being very self-motivated, focused, loving my family but also needing my own interests. Michael and I were very involved in Emmaus once Alyssa was a junior at New Canaan High School, and we were just back from Paris. Emmaus made Michael and I very close and energized our faith. It also helped with our anxieties over our two older children, as did the St. Aloysius prayer group, which I attended often with Alyssa, completing with her the series of talks involved in the program called the Life in the Spirit. I also completed my paralegal certification when Alyssa was in high school. When working full time for three years as a paralegal did not work out, I worked for Jim Talbot, the ophthalmologist, for five years. I was busy, and it made me happy. I had friends from past times but although I had a lot of acquaintances, I did not cultivate close friends in New Canaan except for Judy Boughrum. I was too busy to really spend the time.

Once Alyssa was married, JP in college, Chris on his own, and Will in seventh grade, I entered Pace Law School, dropped out of everything else except family, and gave all my efforts, my best efforts, to my studies. At the very end of the third year it hit, breast cancer, and I crossed over from always good health to big health challenges and issues. It changed me as a person. Along with my focus to concentrate on law school exams, then passing the New York and Connecticut bar exams, I took time to meditate, do yoga, rest, and take naps, help my body with massage and facials. I was lucky for seven years, cancer-free. During that time, I know I slipped a little, becoming competitive, self-centered, and working too many hours. I had to prove myself. Luckily, I told my bosses about the cancer experience before the first recurrence. I had chemotherapy, lost my hair again, wore a wig and shared what I had with my co-workers, but not my clients. Aside from one half-day on for three weeks, with the fourth week off from chemotherapy, I went to the office every day and worked regular hours. I continued working until February 2007, through a second mastectomy, more chemotherapy, radiation, lymphedema, and then breast cancer in the skin. The body can only take so much, and although I absolutely loved my job, my co-workers, and my clients, stress was always a factor as well as my increasing fatigue.

As a result of the intervention of my children at our wonderful 40th wedding anniversary week together in Incline Village, Lake Tahoe, when they said I needed to consider leaving work, I gave it serious thought and realized they were correct. I did not need the stress. I wanted more time to travel, to be with my children, and to concentrate on getting well. That was my turning point. It was the best thing for me. I cultivated close friends, spent more time with my family, spent more time on yoga and Tai Chi and meditation. I became the person I wanted to be. The middle place was over after so many years.

Starting on January 2009 and culminating in the middle of May 2009 with nearly complete dependence, it is now. Many things had to change: my independence, driving a car, my classes outside the home. But I am feeling stronger now, two months later. My children have all come several times and comforted me, loved me, helped me. So many friends have showered their love and concern by emails, phone calls, cards, flowers, and bringing lunch and dinner. My writing is a tremendous means for me to express my feelings and emotions and innermost thoughts. I can truly say life is good.

July 12 – Evening Reflection

Chris and Aidan are on their way back to Colorado. Michael and I are by ourselves tonight. There are no children's visits planned until Jen, Ariana, and Liam come for an overnight the end of July. I wish Alyssa was here with me, but I know she'll be back at some time this summer. At least I hope she will return.

Today was a good day. I had a full night's uninterrupted sleep, draining, shower with Pansy, breakfast, and then a nap on the porch. I had lunch with Chris and Aidan on the porch. I did take a Vicodin because of bad pain in the right hip and left ear. It took a long time to subside. I sat in the family room, and just when I thought I would have to take another Vicodin, the pain eased. Maggie Pierce came with communion, and Sue and Mike Hilgendorff stopped for a short visit on their way back from visiting Sally, Jenna, Suza, and Andy. Chris and Aidan left for the airport with Parks, the driver. Michael and I watched

TV for the first time in ages: the finale of *24*, then the *Fire of Yoga* video. I had a delicious salad with scallops for dinner in the family room, then we drained, wrapped, and got ready for bed. My aches and pains from 8:30 are so much eased now at 9:30, after some Tylenol and sitting in bed, listening to Echoes on the radio. That makes everything seem possible and hopeful. I spoke with JP, Ariana, and Liam but not yet Alyssa and Will.

Tomorrow will be a busy day with the writing group coming at 10:30 am, Holley Egloff with lunch, Sue Lione with dinner, radiation at 2 pm, then Cecelia at 3 pm.

I am letting myself float into the yoga feeling and meditation, looking at my white lotus painting. Whatever sustained stretching and twists I can perform are essential for flexibility, just as meditation is essential to quiet the chatter of the mind. Our hummingbird feeder attracted a hummingbird today. I was so happy to see that, to observe my bird of beauty and good luck. Breathe in and out and relax now. Soon the healing power of sleep will envelop me. Om.

July 14 – Evening Reflection (with Sue Lione)

Today fulfilled its promise of being busy with medical appointments. A welcome surprise was being able to appreciate the comfort of this beautiful day. It started with the ride to Stamford Hospital in the warm sunshine, skies blue with puffy clouds.

Lunch was in the atrium, almost like a secret garden. I left my wheelchair and sat on a wooden chair of the atrium next to the little waterfall, surrounded by lush greenery, my skin tingling and caressed by the gentle sun streaming in.

Once back home, I walked to the patio, sat in my green reclining chair in the shade, but warmed just to the right temperature in the air, while being fanned by a gentle breeze. I reclined back and looked at the perfect light blue of the sky, the various hues of green on the trees and the multiple colors of the flowers on my patio. Occasionally, a bird would fly across or chirp a hello. No hummingbirds came. Perhaps tomorrow, one will appear in the offering of a new day. My eyes grew heavy and closed, and I enjoyed a delicious nap for an hour, reviving me for the afternoon and evening.

I feel like the lotus flower, opening its petals in the muddy water, open to receive and to give love, strength, and beauty.

July 15 – Evening Reflection: Effects of Radiation and Miltex

There are three more days left for my ear radiation. The radiation team is very nice and very efficient. I can't really tell what the true effects are in a positive manner, not yet. I just know that I am very fatigued, probably a cumulative result. The ear hurt enough during the night to warrant a Vicodin. Bactroban and Aquaphor helps keep the skin soothed.

Michael has been applying the Miltex for about three months. While it helped improve the chest and keep it under control in the beginning, some new spots are returning, and the chest has never cleared as before. Once the radiation is over, I will restart taking the VP-16 oral chemotherapy. If that does not work, I really don't know what we will do. This is an opportunity to open my heart even more to receive prayer and trust in Jesus holding me.

My weight went from 210 to 215 in a few days. That is disappointing because I really want to be below 200. I believe it's time to cut back on dessert as I am probably taking in too much sugar and producing too much insulin.

I had good fresh air time today—on the porch with Marion Glennon and Maureen Cozzi, who brought a nice lunch of quinoa and spinach salad. After radiation, I sat on the patio until Jean and Cecilia arrived to do physical therapy with me.

Sue Scannell brought over a delicious dinner, with salmon, asparagus, ratatouille, bread, and salad. Tonight we are Skyping with Alyssa. All in all a good day. Michael saw the hummingbird tonight, but I missed it. Perhaps he or she will visit tomorrow.

Stay positive. Stay focused. Be happy. Smile. Meditate and pray. Nourish the virtues of faith, hope, and charity. Peter Cullen paid a surprise visit today, and Bill Scheyd comes tomorrow, and Ian on Sunday. My priest friends are looking after me.

I dreamed this morning that Alyssa and Laird had twins, one boy and one girl. We shipped out fourteen bottles for draining, stayed in the B&B near their house (no hospital bed), and rented a walker and half step in California. It seems that we visited Will and Sarah, and there was a baby there too. When I relayed my dream to Michael, he said it wasn't really a dream but active day dreaming. It also could be wishful thinking. Why not reach for the stars?

July 18 – Saturday: Feeling Discouraged

My heart is heavy, bearing the burden of a full left lung causing abdominal pressure and increased difficulty breathing. Today we drained three times on the right. I am strongly considering having a catheter put in the left pleural cavity despite its complications of short term—an OR procedure, pain and recovery—and long term: draining maintenance and all that fluid being removed. I would wait until I recovered from the fatigue of radiation, which may take three weeks.

The fatigue can be debilitating, although resting today and draining three times was helpful. I also have a sore left cheek and ear pain. In a way, the worse scenario is the progression of the chest wall with more bumps, open wounds, and pain. I will resume the VP-16 after the last radiation session on Monday. However, the VP-16 was not fighting the chest wall that strongly. What can we switch to that would be more effective and not too strenuous on my body? I don't know. Would it mean going back to Avastin or Exempra? It's a big concern to me.

I have complete dependence, but I need some dignity and comfort for a while. Michael is an extremely kind, patient, and gifted caregiver. I know how hard it must be for him to keep doing this day after day.

What are my choices? Give up or attack each challenge with creativity and hope, thereby creating another new day to enjoy and savor. I can see and spend time with my children and grandchildren, write and paint, and prepare my legacy. I may live long enough to see new grandchildren. That thought keeps me going.

I will take it one day at a time as I always have in the past, with trust in God's help and help from Our Lady of Lourdes. Hope must reign supreme, with faith and love.

July 19 – Reflection on Will's Thought for the Day

All things ebb and flow, today will be better, my outlook and attitude prepare me for the best.

Today is better
Less fatigue
My breathing is less labored,
But we will have to drain three times as we did yesterday

I sat on the porch in the fresh air and sunshine
Had lunch there with Michael
A little nap as well
Then draining #2

Now I'm in the family room, AC on, writing
waiting for visiting nurse Evina and Father Ian

I nurture my inner core, my center
I amass my strength, perseverance, and resolve
I ask for God's protection and grace
I can do what needs to be done, one day at a time

July 19 – Notes from My Children

Will's thought for the day: *You've accomplished the end of radiation. You've accomplished something that seemed impossible only a few weeks ago. With your strength and conviction, anything is possible.*

Alyssa writes often beautiful and encouraging cards, strengthening our bond and even more reminding me of how close we are. The hummingbird in her garden reminds her of the blue and red birds in mine. We are always connected heart and soul. That is true. Her admonition of keep being strong and enjoying every day is true. I know it could be easy to give up, but I won't. I will do it for her, for me, and whatever beautiful events may blossom in the future. I am surrounded by love and prayer. I consciously open my heart to receive all these prayers.

In Will's thought for the day, he reminds me that I finished radiation, something that would have been very difficult a few weeks ago. With my strength and conviction, anything is possible. I am carrying that banner high, waving it in the sun. I am planting it in my garden for one and all to see.

Thank you dear, sweet children.

July 21 – Tuesday: Finished with Radiation

It was good to be finished and not have to travel to the Bennett Cancer Center today. My fatigue now will slowly evaporate, and hopefully my hair will stop falling out. Most of all, the ear will improve. I restart the VP-16 tonight. Hopefully, it will help with the skin on the chest wall, which has slowly worsened even with the Miltex.

I had two deep one-hour naps today and enjoyed Georgia Young's visit, and I finished the Provence landscape. Rita Trieger came and led me in chair yoga and a lotus meditation.

Tomorrow, Ken Dolan will come and lead me in some Tai Chi. I look forward to that.

How am I doing? I am hanging in. It is time to work on "The Quilt of My Life" writing and the "Book of J."

How am I doing? I am hanging in. Not feeling as exhausted as I was last night, I will try to go to bed a little later—9:30 pm instead of 8:30 pm—and sleep through the night rather than waking up at 4 am as I did this morning. No shower planned for tomorrow—just a sponge bath and writing for an hour, then a nap before Gina Barber comes at 11:30 am.

Angie in Rita's yoga class is a Buddhist nun and elder. She and her master, and I believe some others, are doing a four-day prayer and fasting for Michael and me—Saturday to Tuesday. What a rich and wonderful time, with also Jen, Ariana, and Liam visiting on the weekend, and Alyssa coming on Tuesday.

Rita and I meditated on climbing a ladder down into the heart, rung by rung, going deeper into a peaceful place. I could feel it. I was prayerful and powerful. Rita also read a piece on faith, and I could feel that my faith is strong and becomes stronger over time.

For that, I am so grateful.

We also meditated on the lotus flower, slowly opening its petals, growing in beauty and peace as my lotus painting does for me each night before bed, instilling me with quietness and peace.

July 22 – Wednesday: Evening Reflection

So much hurts tonight. It makes me feel sad.

So let's concentrate instead on the positives of today: sitting on the porch in the morning, Gina Barber bringing communion, Mary Runstead having lunch, Ken Dolan coming and doing Tai Chi, Sue Lione visiting and Mary Aldrich too. It was a busy day, and I look forward to a restful and healing sleep. I will open my heart and soul to God's grace. I will meditate on the lotus, opening its petals in trust and faith. I embrace trust and hope and faith. God be with me and hold me. I give myself to your care.

Tomorrow will be a busy day with the visit to Dr. Hall followed by a blood test at Bennett. I thank God for today and for the special love and caring by Michael.

July 23 – Thursday: Transition (with Chris Writing in Colorado)

We have transitions every day: from sleep to awake, from awake to starting our day—what is my plan, what is my schedule for the day? I follow this plan to the best of my ability. It may be having breakfast then exercising or reading or writing. It may be having lunch with a friend who brings lunch for us. It should include a nap. It always includes a shower or sponge bath, usually administered by Caroll, and leg exercises later in the afternoon aided by Cecilia. On some days, there will be Reiki or reflexology, Rita visiting to do yoga, Ken visiting to do Tai Chi, the writing group coming and writing, friends bringing dinner and staying to eat, friends bringing communion, the clergy coming over, Georgia coming to do watercolor with me. I transition from hour to hour, becoming fatigued in the evening but savoring the day and looking forward to a healing night's sleep.

There are my big transitions, my decisions: to undergo ten days of radiation, to take oral chemotherapy, to have a drain inserted in my left pleural cavity. I walk down the road of transitions, breathing deeply, taking in the minute detail of life around me—the flowers of every color, open and welcoming, the light falling on the leaves of the trees and warming the air, and as I walk this road of transition, I am guided by faith, hope, and love.

There is the transition of family visiting, of going from the two of us to the support of family. Transitions are an opportunity for growth.

July 26 – The Next Steps

I don't know what my next big steps will be. I plan to have a left catheter inserted on August 12, but I keep questioning that decision. I would like to take a chemotherapy that will clear up my chest wall and prevent my right ear from getting worse. But I don't know what that is. I am still hoping to arrest this cancer, but it seems to be marching on relentlessly. What next step I can control is to let go of any worry and anxiety, and enjoy every day I do have. To work on strengthening my faith and continue writing, painting, exercising, and doing the things I love that I can do.

I love to visit with my family and friends. I am so appreciative of the love and care directed towards me.

July 28 – Tuesday: Night Time Reflection

After yesterday's darkness and sadness, after the meeting with Bar when he wasn't the usual optimist, I arise from the ashes this morning like a Phoenix. Being extremely tired yesterday was one of the causes of feeling down. Today, I made sure that I slept in later, had a good breakfast, conserved energy by not going upstairs, and took a nice nap on the porch before lunch. Then the day was busy, and there was no afternoon nap. But I watched TV, saw Father Ian and Rita for yoga, and watched TV again after dinner, getting ready for bed and draining. I knew I should be able to bounce back, and I did. I even lifted myself from the green chair this morning and made my way into the kitchen. Each act of self autonomy is very rewarding. I have my new carry bag for my walker, so I can move my own belongings. Caroll's son, Anthony, came and gave me a haircut today. He brought with him Antonio and Francisco, so I had the pleasure of meeting this very nice family. A new visiting nurse caregiver, Alice, came today, and she is very nice. She can do the leg exercises. I look forward to getting into bed soon, prayer, meditation, and a night of healing sleep.

Alyssa arrives tomorrow morning, and a new adventure begins. Must plan an early nap, as it will be a busy day.

It is a new day to love God, love myself, and love others. I will revel in the joy of the closeness of my daughter.

August 1 – A New Month

Here we are, the beginning of August. This Thursday is our 43rd wedding anniversary. I am so happy to be celebrating that wonderful occasion. The possibility that we may go to Bonne Nuit for dinner is phenomenal. I have Alyssa to thank for the planning for that, making a reservation, reserving a wheelchair from Jean, and even a back-up plan of take-out from Bonne Nuit if going out is not feasible. When I reflect on it, it will be early so not crowded, and as far as being concerned how I look, I am what I am. I could wear my wig as my one concession to vanity, or call it dress up and going out, and that would give me a boost. I could keep Tai Chi to 45 minutes and take a short rest afterwards and perhaps even drain at 4:30 pm before going out, so I am not out of breath. That would greatly relieve any anxiety. It sounds like a good plan. It would be a good test. Perhaps then we could even go to the Cattrell wedding on September 26. At least I could plan on doing that.

Today was a glorious day, having a refreshing shower, a large breakfast, then sitting on the porch and having a luxurious sleep. At noon, we were off to Calf Pasture and parked right in front of the beach, viewing the speed boats, sail boats, and kayaks in the water. It was special spending the time with Alyssa and Michael, having a picnic lunch in the car, watching the seaside scene, feeling the warm, gentle breeze blowing in from the water, and inhaling the ocean smells faintly tinged with the odor of sea life. After about an hour, we were back on our way into town and capped off our wonderful excursion with a gelato treat. Back at home, all three of us closed our eyes and fell soundly asleep, Alyssa on the couch next to me and Michael secreted away on the couch in my bedroom. Finally, Alyssa and I are writing together, which we have planned to do since this morning. It is just as well that Georgia did not come to paint in watercolor with me. I realize how important the rest and naps are to my comfort, well-being, and ease of breathing. I must always put that obligation first.

August 5 – Wednesday: On the Eve of our 43rd Wedding Anniversary

Today was a busy day. Up at 6 am, draining, upstairs for shower, breakfast on the porch followed by a one-hour nap before leaving for a CBC at Bennett, taking out lunch from Lemon Grass then eating at Mead Park, a few errands, and then home to drain again and finish lunch. Once again, I had a refreshing nap, followed by leg exercises with Cecelia.

I saw my very fancy wheelchair in the garage. I look forward to going to Bonne Nuit for dinner. I will be fine. What a special 43rd anniversary celebration that will be. I will have a sponge bath to conserve energy, be ready for nap on the porch by 9 am before lunch, Gina, and then Tai Chi with Ken and Susan at 1 pm. Time for another nap before Msgr. Bill Scheyd comes over, and Alice to do the leg exercises. We will drain at 4 pm then the final getting ready touches for dinner and off we go for our 5:30 reservation. I pray for a very restful and healing sleep tonight, and I look forward to a very special day tomorrow.

August 6 – The 43ʳᵈ Wedding Anniversary Celebration (with Alyssa)

Today was a glorious day. The weather was perfect, and I took a nice nap on the porch. Gina came for communion for me and Michael, bringing also a bottle of Veuve Clicquot. Michael served Alyssa, me, and Caroll a delicious lunch: salad with avocado, tomato, cheese, tuna salad, and corn on the cob.

Another nap followed lunch until Ken Dolan and Susan Weiss came for Tai Chi, a rejuvenating session of deep breathing and arm exercises. Alyssa partook with us. Alice came to do leg exercises. We drained, and then Msgr. Scheyd came and gave an anniversary blessing to Michael and me.

Then we started getting ready for our evening out, an anniversary dinner at Bonne Nuit restaurant in New Canaan. I had already applied make-up in the morning. In fact, everyone commented on the make-up and how nice I looked. I was wearing black pants, my blue long sleeved shirt, my pink and purple scarf, and my purple shawl. I put on my fuschia button down shirt, touched up my make-up, Alyssa brought down my wig, and after a glass of white wine and several photos, we were ready to depart for the evening out.

Alyssa had made reservations at the restaurant and also had made arrangements for a lender wheelchair. We parked in the handicapped space on Forest Street, and I was pushed into the restaurant, and the wheelchair fit perfectly at the table, a lovely table for four on the left side of the restaurant directly in front of the window. Alyssa and I started with a glass of Veuve Clicquot and Michael a glass of white wine. A delicious Coquille St. Jacques, grilled scallops served over avocado in an oil and carrot sauce, was shared by Alyssa and me, while Michael had a Caesar salad. For the main course, Alyssa had salmon, Michael had veal, and I had lamb chops served over spinach with a side of pommes frites and asparagus. Alyssa and I shared a glass of Pinot and Michael had a Shiraz. The food was very good, the ambiance fun, and being out was wonderful. Michael won the arm wrestle over whose credit card would be used to pay the bill—his or Alyssa's—and I was wheeled out of Bonne Nuit to the gelato store for some vanilla-chocolate gelato to wash down my pills. We ate in the little garden next to the gelato store, and it was delightful to savor this wonderful evening. Finally, we left for the ride back home where we immediately undertook our usual nighttime procedures.

What a day. Truly a day to remember.

August 7 – Friday: A Love Note to my Daughter

I just read the message on your beautiful magnolia card. I cherish your words. I love you, and I miss being with you. I know we both have work to do, and that we can't always do it sitting side by side. I worry about your Achilles tendon, but it was funny having another handicapped person in the house. It forced you to slow down, take it easy, and both of us spent time together with legs elevated.

You are beautiful, talented, compassionate, kind, giving, caring, and loving. You fill me with joy and hope. You are the nourishment for me, bearing the magnolia flower. That is such a beautiful card you gave me. It must be an exquisite painting. I will keep the card next to my bed so that I can read it every night before I go to sleep until I see you again.

I will keep the mini quilt in my journal to remind me to keep working on the "Quilt of My Life," so that it can go into production and reflect a finished project as does this mini quilt.

I have shared so openly with you. You have seen my ups and downs and shepherded me through them. We are as close and comfortable with each other as body and soul can possibly exist.

My darling daughter, may you be transfigured with light and filled with health and healing. May God always hold you close and your angels protect you. My love is always with you.

August 9 – Flowers

As I sit at the kitchen table looking through the large sliding glass door into the patio or outside on the patio or on the glassed-in sun porch overlooking the patio, I see all the colorful flowers of what I call my secret garden. There are potted plant flowers of all shapes and varieties, multi-layered on tables and chairs and clustered together for maximum color effect and aesthetic beauty. Many plants have personal significance: the large plant with ever blooming purple flowers sent by a friend; the pink and red geraniums and white flowers planted by my sister-in-law, Patty; the large arrangement of red, blue, and yellow flowers bought by my son, Jean-Paul; the beautiful rose plant sent by my yoga class, a beautiful large pink and yellow rose now open like a lotus flower to receive the sun and offer peace and pleasure to the eye; the pink geraniums and impatiens my husband bought; and the large rose and white fuchsia plant that our daughter, Alyssa, gave us for our anniversary last week, overflowing the hanging basket, laden with flowers to attract my favorite hummingbird. I enjoy these flowers every day and am soothed by their beauty.

It reminds me of gardens I have seen on my travels, small gardens and very large gardens. When we lived in Versailles from 1972-1977, we often visited the Chateau and walked through paths with thousands of small plantings, very carefully arranged and displayed. Every season the plants would dry up and others were inserted so that there was a perpetual beautiful mosaic of color and careful design.

In 1999, we traveled with Hans, Anne, and Johan, then just a year old, to Vancouver, British Columbia, Canada, and visited the Butchart Gardens with acres of landscaped gardens, paths winding through exotic green plants, and bright and varied flowers. We visited the main house and gift shop, and bought cards with pictures of the gardens. The cards are all gone now, sent on various occasions to treasured family and friends.

When Alyssa and Laird were in graduate school in the 1990's, we went to see the lilac festival in a park near their apartment. Lilac trees of every species and size, and blossoms of all colors of lilac and white, covered the hills of the park, spectacularly showing off their beauty. Rhododendron plants with fuchsia, lavender, and white flowers joined the chorus of color.

In May 2005, I traveled with Michael, Will, and Sarah to France, and we spent a day in Giverny, Monet's house and gardens. We walked over arched bridges, spanning ponds crowded with lily pads, with lotus blossoms of every hue of lavender, pink, and white, all breathtakingly beautiful. We meditated on these blossoms for a long time, reluctantly pulling ourselves away, visiting the gift shop and buying a print of the beautiful lily scene.

In Barbados, Michael and I visited the beautiful gardens of the manor house where one could go for tea. In Bermuda, red bougainvillea and other blossoms filled the large shrubs six feet tall lining the sides of the narrow road from the airport to town and the resorts, which one could travel to only by motorbike or by taxi on the two-lane roadway.

In Caneel Bay, St. John's, British Virgin Islands, large pink and fuchsia flowers covered the rich foliage on the many landscaped paths.

In my daughter's cottage at Half Moon Bay, California, flowers of every description line the borders of her garden, pink and lavender hydrangeas, rose and white fuchsia, pink roses, red poppies, white and burgundy calla lilies, and pink bougainvillea.

Every week my husband buys me roses: red, pink, orange, and white, which adorn the kitchen table, bringing the aesthetic beauty inside. Friends bring flowers, roses, mixed bouquets, sunflowers, dahlias, and orchids which grace the family room and porch.

Each flower has a different structure which I study carefully when I am painting a watercolor with flowers. Roses, orchids, hydrangeas, geraniums, and freesia, all have their own geometric shapes expressing the diversity and creativity God gave us in nature.

Being observant and taking time to pause, study, and reflect is one way to appreciate and take advantage of this free gift to us.

August 12 – Dishes

Every night, we use our white Limoges plates which I bought at the Marche in Versailles in 1973. They are our everyday dishes and have lasted all these years except for a few thrown out because of chips. Michael loves serving dinner on white plates, and of course they go with everything. It is amazing how durable and elegant they are. For salad plates, I have a beige and brown flower design by Villeroy and Boch which I bought in the 1980's on sale because they were a discontinued pattern. To supplement, I bought some pure white salad plates which better matched the Limoges. So a pattern continues, including blue and white check, and brown and white check, tablecloths and matching napkins which I also bought in Versailles many years ago in the 1970's.

To be festive, or when guests come, we often use our Villeroy and Boch plates with a botanical pattern. What I love is that each plate has a different flower and therefore blues, reds, purples, greens, and yellows enliven our table. These plates were ordered in Paris before our return home in 1985, and I ordered plates in every size, many accessory dishes, coffee mugs, coffee pot, tea pot, sugar, and creamer. What a wise purchase: so practical, durable, yet sturdy and used so often. It completely fills the shelves of my antique china hutch with four old glass panels, stationed across from the kitchen table.

More fragile but beautiful is my cream and green Moustiers faience dishware, with each plate depicting a different male or female courtesan. These plates should be washed by hand and handled carefully so they don't chip. Since I love them so much, I have to ask Michael if we can use them more often for dinner for the two of us. They are antique. Some were purchased in Paris and others were found in some specialty stores in the US.

Then there is the gold and white china from my mother with the matching glasses with gold rims. I do not think that the china is of great value, and some of the dishes have broken, but it has great sentimental value. I often used it at holiday time with the children. Will, the most sentimental of my children, has requested that this service be given to him at the proper time, and it shall be together with the glasses.

Our best china is a service for eight of the Royal Doulton English bone china pattern English Renaissance. It is a beautiful white plate with light green trim overlaid with a gold design. They of course should be washed by hand, and we do not use them very often. Margie and Art Jones gave us two place settings for our wedding and the rest we bought in London during our time in France.

So completes our repertoire of dishes, each set carrying a beautiful memory with it, uniting the past with the present.

August 24 – Monday: The Need for a Good Cry (with JP)

I remember Grandmother telling me that she could not produce tears because her tear ducts were dry. My eyes have the opposite problem: my eyes always have tears rolling down, especially when I am in bed.

Everyone knows I cry at sentimental times, telephone commercials, and scenes to end movies.

When my mother died, I cried for hours and probably for days afterwards.

But I can't recall having a good cry afterwards, not because of pain, frustration, or anger. I have had tears of joy, at a child's wedding, seeing a grandchild, or been moved by a beautiful event.

But just as crying is healthy and so is laughter, I don't do enough. I am too serious, too intense, which I compensate for or alleviate by meditation, visualization, and anxiety and stress reduction.

Although I did cry when I heard that Karen had cancer, I did not cry over my own diagnosis, nor my concerns, nor my surgery and treatments, nor a lower law school grade than I anticipated. I am trying to figure out why, and can't. Is it good or bad, I don't know. If I did cry, I should by crying my eyes out today or when, on May 18, I met with Dr. Bar and he said I have one to three weeks to live. Perhaps the reason is that I have faith, and faith gives love and hope. There is no reason for crying in this case. From that perspective, I am lucky. And in so writing this, I have been able to figure out what I could not before.

Writing brings out the truth and allows you to love fully and to focus on that wisdom.

August 25 – Tuesday: The Intruder (with JP)

In 1995, when I was finishing law school, I was quite excited. I knew that Dad and Judy Boughrum were planning a surprise party as a celebration.

On May 1, I was diagnosed with breast cancer. I was shocked because I was always so healthy. Dr. Ponn called me in Janet Johnson's law school office where I worked doing research for her. I did not go to my last class, but came home. Will was home. I told him and said not to worry, that I would be fine. He was only in ninth grade. I told Dad when he came home several hours later from work. He said she must have made a mistake. It couldn't be. The only person I called was my friend Elaine Harris. Her husband was a pediatrician and a brain cancer survivor. He arranged for a CT scan and a bone scan the next day. He went to the Bennett Cancer Center and saw both Dr. Lo and Dr. Bar. After thinking about it for a day, Elaine felt that Michael Bar would be the best doctor for me and called him so that he would see me that week, which he did. She kept telling me, "You are going to be fine. Just take it one baby step by baby step."

Dad spoke with the family, and I was able to concentrate on tests, surgery, and graduation. I told them I did not want too much medication, and my surgeon agreed. She said I was her attorney, and we had to keep me well and going. Because of all that happened, I did not consider cancer an intruder but an inconvenience, something I had to deal with. I was worried and nervous, but I had a lot to focus on— my law work. I graduated, started chemo and studying for the bar exam. Sometimes I was very sick. I went to Albany, New York, with shots of Neupogen to administer.

I passed the New York and Connecticut bar exams. Taking the exams was against Dr. Bar's wishes, but I said I would be fine, and if not I would come home. At Elaine's arrangement, I had a massage once a week, took vitamins from her doctor, and went through the chemo. There is more to write about but that is the synopsis. It was long but worked, and once the chemo was over, I started chest wall radiation. I did everything I could, as aggressive as I could, and I was lucky.

August 25 – Meditation (with JP)

One big impact of clearing my mind is that I am becoming better at meditation. I often try to reach that state, but it is not easy. For that reason, I felt that tonight's meditation exercise, led by JP, was excellent. Only at one point did I wonder how much time had passed, but then it did not enter my mind and the time passed quickly. I felt what really helped, in addition to picturing an empty room, was to take breaths. Breaths in and out while not saying picture your breath or breathe in and out. I believe the deep breathing reminded me of Jean who is always asking me if I do it every day.

I am honest and tell her even although it is easy for me, that do I forget or am lazy about it. I know from yoga and Tai Chi how important it is to take deep breaths. I don't know why I don't do it regularly during the day—I am crazy. I have to fix it in my mind and do it.

I thought of JP because he was the impetus for this prompt as for many other things which help me and I am so proud and so happy for that.

August 26 – Reality, Joy, Meditation (with JP)

Reality
Joy
Meditation

I just don't know why those three words came into my head. But here is what I think, these may be the reasons.

I must always face the reality of a situation and not delude myself to think it is something else.

I must always be joyful. In this case, I must convince myself even if I am feeling low or not feeling well. Of course, it is important to recognize the actual feelings or symptoms, acknowledge, and let them register for a few hours or a day if needed. But then it has to be over.

Meditation, along with prayer, is important, necessary, and healthy for me, preferably every day. I try to meditate once during the day for a few minutes and before going to sleep at night. I am usually asleep halfway through it which is good. My meditation is not necessarily clearing my mind, but picturing a bright white light entering my body through my head and watching it as it brushes the cells in my body, lingering especially where I know cancer cells may be present. It feels very enforcing and very healing.

August 28 – What Are Big Girls Made of (with Writing Group)

(I am not feeling well today; have to use my oxygen)

I believe everyone is different with a different personality. Unless one is very insecure and completely dependent on her mother, sister, or friend, women have different personalities. This is a function of one's upbringing, environment, and preferences. In addition to her body and personality, each woman has a mind and a free will. This is not designed by her, it just exists.

In my stage of life, my soul is more important to me than my body. At my death, my body will remain behind but my soul will be me. God is a perfect spirit and to be with God, we must be a perfect spirit and love God above all else. The soul may take years to cleanse in Purgatory, my priest advisor tells me. He says that my suffering is purifying my soul now, and that I am making saints of people that willingly perform corporal works of mercy by either visiting or bringing lunch and dinners or sending cards and flowers.

Of course, all these thoughts and suggestions must be taken on faith. We do not know for sure; no one does. But it is much stronger for me to believe it than nothing. It gives me a beautiful afterlife to consider. I have faith every day that I will be better, that the day will be good, and that I will have a good day. My faith engenders joy and hope.

Of all the mysteries of life, the soul is the biggest one. I also know that to continue on every day I depend on the grace and strength from God.

No doubt this help comes in the form of my wonderful caregivers, my husband and children, Caroll, Anita, and the others. What would I do without them?

September 2 – Commitment, Love, Desire (with Alyssa)

All my actions are driven by love, love of self and love of others. For example, when faced with leaving to stay at hospice, I said no not because I don't love and honor Michael, but because it would not be what I love to do. At this point, I can't be manipulated. I have a commitment to myself to try my best, give it everything I have and succeed. I want to be in my own home, in my own chair or bed, surrounded by my surroundings, loved ones, and friends. My desire is to live for as long as possible. My intense desire is to see Alyssa have a baby as well as Will and Sarah. These things don't happen overnight.

If I don't survive that, I have been working with Father Ian on purifying my soul, so I am ready for my final stage. I feel comfortable with that. My desire at that time would be to have all my children with me at the end.

I know it will be hard to say goodbye, but I believe there will be grace in the next life and that my memory will carry on and continue in my children and grandchildren.

September 5 – Being Outside (with Alyssa)

I have a lot of tools to keep me cope. I have my mind and my memory and my soul. As I rest and get stronger, I can mobilize again, go up the stairs in the hallway, back into the wheelchair. I can get out of the wheelchair and rest in the brown chair. These are things I love to do.

I can continue to enjoy and reflect on the beautiful flowers. Michael again brought beautiful flowers for the room.

I am here with Alyssa.
Praise You Lord Jesus.

September 8

Joan M. O'Brien passed away peacefully on September 8, 2009, surrounded by her family in the home she loved.

CHAPTER 7 –
"THE BOOK OF J": SPIRITUAL REFLECTIONS & WRITING PROMPTS

God Be With Me and Hold Me

I will open my heart and soul to God's grace.
I will meditate on the lotus,
Opening its petals in trust and faith.
I embrace trust and hope and faith.
God be with me and hold me.
I give myself to your care.

These Moments are My Divine Gifts

There is always a blessing
The hand of God extending love in
Unexpected ways
My soul being purified
My body resting and refreshed
My heart open and soaring with love
Today, these moments are my divine gifts

Open to Prayer

May each day be like a prayer, thoughtful and pure
Filled with compassion and love
May each day remind me of the miracle of my life.

God the Creator

This is the opening of the art hanging at the New Canaan YMCA. I wish I could attend these events, but that is not possible at this time. The site of my catheter hurts today. Michael said it does not look red. Luckily I see Dr. Hall tomorrow. It makes me ponder what direction to go with the left side. It is good that there are still decisions I can make for myself, as hard as they may be.

Have I not turned everything over to God? God doesn't say to give up, just to trust and have faith, hope, and love.

It is my faith to believe that I am important to God, just as He mentions the lilies in the field. I am a micro speck in God's big creation. Look at a blade of grass as it trembles with life, making chlorophyll to stay green, housing worms, ants, beetles, soil microorganisms. Go down within the green, the soothing color. Add a dash of yellow and it turns blue, add a dash of red and it turns purple. So our lives turn, so easily.

(June 15, 2009)

Based on Joan's writing, here is a writing prompt on God:

Think about when you could not attend an event because of illness. Write about it and how you felt. Imagine, in your mind, turning it over to God. Write about God's love and care for you.

Original watercolor by Joan M. O'Brien, 2008

Pilgrimage

You are invited to go on a pilgrimage to Lourdes, France. You are excited. It is someplace you always wanted to visit. The day of departure arrives: April 29, 2008. You are the "malade" and your husband is accompanying you as caregiver. A huge chartered plane, World Airlines, transports 380 passengers, pilgrims, directly from Newark airport to Lourdes. The anticipation is heavy. No miracles are expected, but a profound experience is—a quickening of the heart and soul, a deepening of faith. Long lines through customs at the airport.

(May 8, 2009)

Based on Joan's writing, here is a writing prompt on a journey:

Write about a journey of faith that you have taken. How did you feel before going? What were the preparations? Why was this a special trip for you? Write about your pilgrimage.

Joan and Michael on a pilgrimage to Lourdes, 2008

Trip to Lourdes – April 30 to May 6, 2008

I was honored to be sponsored and then accepted to make a Pilgrimage to Lourdes as a "malade" on this Jubilee year, the 150th anniversary of the apparition of Our Lady to Bernadette Soubirous in the Grotto at Lourdes, with Michael coming as my caregiver. I was one of 49 malades in a group of 420 people comprised of members and volunteers of Malta USA. The Order of Malta is a lay religious order dedicated to serving the sick and poor and defending the Catholic faith.

I knew that the theme of this 23rd annual Order of Malta Pilgrimage was "Sent to Love and Serve." My expectation for the Pilgrimage was to experience everything Lourdes offered, and my hope was for spiritual rekindling. The Pilgrimage far exceeded my expectation and hope. The beauty of Lourdes, and the awe and emotion I felt, were absolutely enhanced by the outpouring of love, caring, and dedication of the Knights and Dames of Malta.

The site of the apparition of Our Lady to Bernadette in the Grotto has been expanded into an area called the "Domaine." It comprises the Rosary Basilica, the Basilica of the Immaculate Conception, the Grotto, the Baths, the Church of St. Bernadette, the Pius X Basilica, and several other buildings. It is very impressive and beautiful. Our five days in Lourdes were very well organized and full of activities from morning to evening. Eventually, I became familiar with all aspects of the Domaine. The love and dedication of the Knights and Dames of Malta, medical personnel, and volunteers to the malades and to each other was just incredible. I traveled in a "voiture" pulled by my Knight, Orly Benedict, and pushed by my Dame, Marion Glennon, who never left my side. They were always so solicitous as was every other person. At every assembling, the malades in the voitures took front place. I remember my first day, Thursday morning, being pulled into the Basilica of the Rosary, and my eyes filling with tears at the beauty of the mosaic on the ceiling, a mosaic of Mary as Queen, with the words "To Jesus through Mary."

My most memorable experience was on Friday, our second day in Lourdes. A Morning of Recollection was led by Monsignors Sheehan and Wallen who each gave beautiful homilies which encouraged reflection on who we are, what are we doing for others, and how we are taking the time to pause and reflect. In the afternoon, I went to the baths with my host, Marion. I was brought into a room with five other people. Two volunteer women helped me undress and held a sheet around me. Then I was brought into a room partitioned off from the dressing room. A bath tub filled with water from the stream was in the center of the room. Four volunteers took off my blue sheet and wrapped me in a white one which was also wet and freezing cold. A statue of Mary was at the head of the bath. The women lowered me into the water, and I bathed for a moment in the very cold spring water. It was very emotional for me. And when they lifted me up I was not cold, and when they took off the sheet and replaced it with my original one, I was nearly dry. I call that my pre-healing. I experienced a healing of body, mind, heart, and soul that afternoon at the mass of healing and anointing at St. Bernadette's Church. That evening at dusk I participated in the candlelight procession, pulled in my voiture through the Domaine, holding my lit candle and seeing thousands of people either processing as well or lining the way or standing up high on the ramparts, all joining in one voice saying the rosary and singing "Ave Maria." It was the most incredible experience I ever had and the strongest profession of faith I have ever seen. At the end of the candlelight procession, at nearly 11 pm, four of us went to the Grotto. Many people were kneeling at the entrance to the Grotto waiting for mass to begin. It was an atmosphere of hushed reverence. Someone told my charioteer to take me into the Grotto by the handicapped/malade entrance. There a ramp allowed him to pull my voiture into the heart of the Grotto. There was the spring that has been flowing since the time Bernadette dug in the dirt. Many people leave flowers or photos at this site. I had prepared a little pink silk purse with personal items that represented all of my life, and, in particular, articles that related to sadness or grief and articles that related to my illness. I wanted to leave all these tangible items and the cellular memories that they represented with Our Lady of Lourdes and thereby wash myself clean.

On each of the following days, mass was held in a different location: The Grotto, the Pius X Basilica filled to its 30,000 capacity with Malta members from all over the world, and the Basilica of the Immaculate Conception. Interspersed with the spiritual was the camaraderie, the growing friendships, the sharing over meals at D'Espagne and Mediterranee, and the final late cappuccino or glass of wine at an outside table overlooking the river Gave. These are the memories of my Lourdes Pilgrimage I want to share and to always remember.

(May 2008; reprinted from Publication in Knights of Malta Journal)

Based on Joan's writing, here is a prompt on a spiritual place:

Think about a time when you were at a spiritual place. Describe the people and the place in vivid detail. Then, write about how it felt. What were your experiences? Did you have any moments of healing or insight? Write them to remember them. Write about your experiences at a spiritual place.

Gathering at the Grotto in Lourdes

Being Carried – The Voiture

When I first arrived in Lourdes on May 1, 2008, I arrived as a blank slate, knowingly willing to absorb all experiences nonjudgmentally and to open the pores of my body, my very cells, like newly hatched baby birds in a nest, to be filled with the scent of the Pyrenees, the energy of thousands of pilgrims, and the visual impact of the Domaine that is Lourdes consisting of the Grotto, the Baths, the Basilicas, and churches.

I experienced everything in the cocoon of my voiture, a cart pulled by one person and pushed by another from behind. The first day of arrival, I was pulled through the town crowded with many pilgrims to celebrate the 150th anniversary of the apparitions of Mary, the mother of God, to Bernadette Soubirous, a simple shepherd girl.

The voiture parted the sea of people. Sometimes the wheels came very close to those walking and even a few feet were run over, making me worry about being a malade creating other malades. Thankfully, there was no serious damage. My charioteer became more skillful at maneuvering the voiture, and I relaxed and felt every emotion layer upon me in my cocoon. Instead of making my way through crowds on foot, I avoided fatigue and distraction and could only feel awe. I was in the moment, each moment. Spontaneously, tears would come to my eyes and feelings of hope, love, and joy. As if looking through a telescope in my vehicle, I saw individuals, the Knights and Dames of Malta, the auxiliary members, the volunteers, and even the other malades, each showing by their actions service, love, charity, goodness, warmth.

I don't know if I received the miracle of physical healing, but I know that I received healing at a cellular level. Whatever hurt, grief, or resentment I may have carried in my cells during my life is gone. I feel a lightness, a peace, a hope, and love. I was washed in the waters of the baths, the water flowing from the grotto, and my soul is shining brightly as one perfect white candle. I know I can keep this feeling even now outside of my voiture.

(May 2008; originally published as "The Voiture: From the Inside Out" in Knights of Malta Journal)

Based on Joan's writing, here is a prompt on being carried:

Write about an experience of being carried, or an experience of being cared for while you experienced healing. Perhaps you might recall an experience of purification, when you traded hurt, grief, and resentment for lightness, peace, hope, and love. Or perhaps you might remember an experience of quiet healing, in body, mind, or spirit. Write about what happened and how it made you feel. Write about healing as you were being carried.

Joan in her voiture, 2008

Healing

Yesterday I was invited to a mass of anointing and healing at St. Michael's parish in Greenwich, Connecticut. The invitation was issued by the Knights of Malta who took me on the inspiring trip to Lourdes, France, in May. As I traveled the Merritt Parkway, I marveled in the beauty of the sun filtering through multi-colored leaves. The landscape was so soothing, so beautiful. I thought was a nice prelude to what was to come.

The pastor of St. Michael's in Greenwich is a good friend of mine. Although he has been pastor for over a year, I never went to mass at his church. What a lovely church it is. Rustic in contrast to gothic or grand. The floor to ceiling windows invite nature to come in. I felt warm and comfortable, seeing the sun and leaves of gold, orange, red, and green. My friend sitting next to me reminded me that you get two wishes when you are in a new church, so I quickly made those wishes.

It was a good feeling to be back among some of the malades, caregivers, and leaders who were with me in Lourdes. Msgr William who celebrated the mass gave a powerful homily and laid his hands on each malade and touched us with holy oil.

Noticeably missing were those no longer with us. My good friend, Julia Arliss from New Canaan, died in June. Another friend, Tina, also died in June. We were all malades together in Lourdes. One of the child malades died in October. We prayed for those not with us and celebrated the life of those who were. That is all we can do.

We go on, each day a new day, each day healing our souls, our emotions, and our bodies in whatever way we can.

(October 27, 2008)

Based on Joan's writing, here is a writing prompt on healing:

Think about a particular experience of healing. Where and when did it take place? Who was present and what rituals were involved? Describe in details what happened and how you felt about this healing. Open yourself to healing, and let the words flow forth.

Faith

My faith is again a stronger element in my life, a conscious acknowledgement of my acceptance and my willingness to nurture it in my life. Faith, hope, and love are the three cardinal virtues. I have concentrated more on love and hope.

During radiation when I am lying on the table, my head is just slightly elevated, bolster under knees, head turned to the side patiently waiting as they set the precise alignment for the electron beams. Then they are set, and some material is placed over my ear and part of my face to absorb some of the electron rays. My forehead is taped to this material and then to the table. My chin is taped in the same way. Then they leave the room, and I am left alone. Although it is not long, I feel alone. I ask Jesus to hold me in his arms. I ask God the Father to be merciful and God the Holy Spirit to bestow his gift of healing upon me. I ask our Lady of Lourdes to protect me. This prayer gives me peace and enables me to relax, to breathe, to relax my hips, which are aching, and to calm my breathing. Then the technicians are back, take off the tape and material, move the machine, and sit me up. Another session is over.

I have nurtured my faith by inviting over Father Ian, Msgr. Peter Cullen, and Msgr. Bill Scheyd. I discuss with each one what they think Heaven is like and how is one prepared to cross over. They each have a different perspective and are honest with me. The older priests share their life experiences and their sense of humor.

Gina Barber and my friends bring me the Eucharist to fill my cells with grace and strength. Enjoying each day, the beauty of nature, the variation and color of flowers, sharing with friends, and feeling the warmth and unconditional love of my family are all gifts of faith.

I bless this day of faith and am grateful for it.

(July 9, 2009)

Based on Joan's writing, here is a writing prompt on faith:

When have you needed faith most? Write about an experience when faith helped you. Use concrete detail to describe where you were, what happened, and how you felt. Write about the power and meaning of faith in your life.

Original watercolor by Joan M. O'Brien, 2009

Hope

What is hope? Hope is eternal. It is the sunlight, the caress, the smile, the drive to keep going, to stay strong, to be positive.

Sharon Bray wrote, "We face the reality we've been dealt, and we turn our hope into clearly achievable goals." Have I faced the reality I've been dealt? Not really. First of all, the reality keeps changing and, secondly, I keep hoping for a "cure" outcome. This is not a criticism of myself. It is just me looking at the situation with eyes wide open. My reality is fuzzy, hazy, an impressionistic painting, but my life is clear, defined, strong. Being goal-oriented I can channel my hope into clearly definable goals. I have to credit people in my life for helping me define those goals.

Two years ago my son, Jean-Paul, came to visit from Colorado in April. I had just had surgery and was living day to day, surviving day to day. He said, "Mom, you need to set goals for yourself: three-month, one-year and three-year goals." We talked through it, and I did come up with goals. He came back in June for my birthday and had these goals printed up and framed to remind me. Yes, I am achieving these goals or at least trying.

But accepting the reality and working and planning and setting goals for the particular reality is a bigger challenge. When I was in the hospital last week my son, Will, came from California. He is my cheerleader as well as my technical support. Through his efforts I have a new computer. Instead of waiting twenty minutes to open a program and crashing constantly, I can now be online efficiently. Of course, I need the computer in the implementation of my goals.

Here are my goals: to become active in an organization such as lymphedema and cancer; to be a writer and a speaker; to help others.

But how do I translate my reality into hope? I hope for quality of life, for a long life. Specifically, I have to change so many things to accommodate my reality. Can I do it? I hope I can.

I realize that I must set goals to help myself: health-related, taking-care-of-myself goals to help myself. How can I accept an invitation to a formal Christmas dance when my feet are so swollen that I can't wear nice dress shoes? Is this a big deal? No. But how do I deal with it specifically? Ignore it or what? This I realize is my current challenge. I am changing physically and have to adapt to that mentally.

I do have hope. I know I will always have hope.

Now is the time to work out the plan, make the decisions, and keep letting the sun shine in.

(November 7, 2008)

Based on Joan's writing, here is a writing prompt on hope:

How can you turn hope into clearly achievable goals? First write about the struggle you are facing right now, and then write about your goals. Set three-month, one-year, and three-year goals. Write them out, print them and frame them so you can see them. Then write how it feels to turn hope into goals—how is the sun shining for you now?

Original watercolor by Joan M. O'Brien, 2008

Spirituality

How do I relate it all together? I was brought up Catholic with 16 years of formal Catholic education. My faith was nurtured by the traditions and rituals, and my mind assured by the theology courses with proofs of God's existence, enhanced by the rhetoric of Thomas Aquinas, St. Augustine, and many others. The changes in custom made by the Vatican II Council encouraged laity involvement and even more personal interaction. For so many years, I prayed to Jesus and his mother, Mary, for guidance, and it was always forthcoming.

I have a friend who lost her husband to cancer, and she turned away from God, actually blamed God for her loss. I would ask myself how she could carry on without her faith.

When I was first diagnosed with cancer, I belonged to a prayer group who prayed over me, some people speaking in tongues. I credit their gift of healing as a large factor in my seven and a half years of being cancer-free.

But prayers are not always answered. Children die, friends die, recurrence happens. Now what? Believe harder, try harder? Tap into the energy of the universe with meditation, peace, and positive thinking? In Tai Chi, we move Chi, positive energy, gently through our bodies. I have done all these things.

But my soul must be nourished also. I realize that I am perhaps angry with God for some hard times these past two years. I also realize that my faith encourages me to be a good person, kind and loving to others and to myself. My faith is important and must be nurtured.

I feel like I am also wandering down a new road again. I am confused. This Wednesday is Ash Wednesday, the beginning of Lent. I can take this period of Lent as my time to pray, reflect, and listen. My hope is for joy, strength, rebirth, and renewed faith. Lord, show me the way. I can't do it by myself.

(February 23, 2009)

Based on Joan's writing, here is a prompt on spirituality:

Write about your own spiritual journey. What were the most formative experiences shaping your faith? When was your faith tested? When did you have a crisis in your spirituality? Where are you now on your spiritual path? Write about your spirituality and where you are now. End with a prayer to God about what you need right now.

Hallelujah

We listened to the Leonard Cohen song "Hallelujah" and read the lyrics. Although the words were not uplifting to me, the word Hallelujah is and means "Praise Yahweh." In the Christian tradition, we use the word Alleluia to mean praise God. I often use the word in a congratulatory mode or to express a feeling of wonder, beauty, or insight.

Yesterday, I had a long conversation with my son, Chris, who just concluded eight days of a Lakota Indian celebration in northern Colorado called Sundance. The entire focus was on prayer for others, and a self-awakening and opening oneself to the spirit versus the mind or body. It included four days of preparation and praying in a sweat lodge and four days of dancing in the sun starting each day at sunrise and ending each day at sunset in a sweat lodge praying while fasting completely from food and water during the four days. The experience and level he attained were so completely fulfilling to him, and he said he prayed for me constantly.

He prayed for peace and comfort, for endurance, and for the knowledge and affirmation to love myself and to tell myself these words. It was a beautiful sharing. He knew that I had been praying for him, and he felt that. I asked him why, with all his prayer, I have such a terrible stomach ache all day Tuesday. Maybe he did pray, because I am so much better today.

For several years, Michael and I participated in a spiritual weekend retreat for high school students called Emmaus. The weekend lasted from Friday afternoon to Sunday evening and was filled with liturgies, including mass; talks given by clergy, adults, and teens; much singing; good food; and beautiful services called Tenebrae and Agape.

Tenebrae started with creation and in song took us through the crucifixion and resurrection of Jesus. In Agape, we broke bread and shared it with each other, speaking of Agape love, an unconditional love. All this intensity and limited sleep produced a euphoric religious high among everyone. We had a beautiful community of love and support and faith in God. We have seen many Emmaus miracles of teens who were lost and confused who then found themselves.

When Chris told me about the Sundance festival, he likened it to an Emmaus experience as the closest analogy he could make. Hallelujah to both. Hallelujah to love, spirit, faith, and the ability of each person to transcend to a higher spiritual level.

(August 12, 2009)

Based on Joan's writing, here is a prompt on Hallelujah:

Write about your Hallelujah and the people who share hallelujahs. What experiences have you had and how did they make you feel? What does Hallelujah mean to you? What do you need to praise today?

Prayer

Will's thought for the day today was that I should be mindful of prayer—the prayer of family and friends for me along with the love and care that accompanies this prayer, and that it has been an important ingredient in my endurance of treatment and everyday challenges. That is very true and a very good reminder. While I have consciously opened myself to healing energy, Chris' long distance treatments, Katherine's Reiki, and Deb's reflexology, I have not opened my heart to prayer. Yes, I am very grateful for it, but I realize I must consciously open my heart and my pores so the grace of prayer can flow in easily. It is prayer from so many people, their daytime and night prayer, their rosaries, masses said for me by my priest friends.

I am thinking of the tremendous flow of grace and strength and holiness that can fill me, like a swollen river rushing to a new height and carrying fertile soil in its deposits. There have been studies and positive published reports on the power of prayer, one's own personal prayer and prayer said by another on a person's behalf. I open myself to prayer, to love of God. I open myself to receive.

Bestow on me, Holy Spirit, your gifts of healing.
Have mercy on me, God the Father.
Wrap me in your arms and carry me, Jesus, God the Son.

Our Lady of Lourdes, pray for me.
Continue to instill in me the peace and beauty of Lourdes,
The grotto, the baths, the beautiful music in your church.

Pray for me, family and friends
I am ready to receive the strength and grace you send.
I am ready to learn to appreciate and to accept.

May each day be like a prayer, thoughtful and pure
Filled with compassion and love
May each day remind me of the miracle of my life.

(July 10, 2009)

Based on Joan's writing, here is a writing prompt on prayer:

Write about being open to prayer. Who has been praying for you or sending healing energy? Name them and thank them. Then, open yourself to prayer. Describe how it feels in your body to be open to prayer. End by writing a prayer for yourself.

Meditation

Reality, Joy, Meditation. I just don't know why those three words came into my head. But here is what I think, these may be the reasons.

I must always face the reality of a situation and not delude myself to think it is something else.

I must always be joyful. In this case, I must convince myself even if I am feeling low or not feeling well. Of course, it is important to recognize the actual feelings or symptoms, acknowledge, and let them register for a few hours or a day if needed. But then it has to be over.

Meditation, along with prayer, is important, necessary, and healthy for me, preferably every day. I try to meditate once during the day for a few minutes and before going to sleep at night. I am usually asleep halfway through it which is good. My meditation is not necessarily clearing my mind, but picturing a bright white light entering my body through my head and watching it as it brushes the cells in my body, lingering especially where I know cancer cells may be present. It feels very enforcing and very healing.

(August 26, 2009)

Based on Joan's writing, here is a prompt on meditation:

Close your eyes, take three deep breaths, and then open your mind to listen to what three words come into your head. Write them down, and then write about them. How do those words speak to you, spiritually? Write about your experience and the feelings that come from those three words. Write as a form of meditation. Write about how meditation works for you and your body. Write about meditation, and write as a form of healing meditation.

Perseverance

On my birthday, Will wished me peace, love, and hope. They are beautiful virtues. I want to embrace them. Tonight I need perseverance and grace. Perseverance to help breathing, evenly in and out until it becomes smoother. The grace to do this without a lot of flailing and attention. It is so hard, and I know how supportive Michael and Alyssa are with me tonight.

So let me take myself on a journey, a Bernie Siegel journey to a castle where there is a strong box filled with all the tools I need to ride this out. I know it still may be uncomfortable, but it will be better after tomorrow, and our plan after that will help me ride this out.

Take me deep into dream land to walk in fields of flowers in the sunlight, to sit on a daisy flower, to feel the touch of butterflies and the kiss of the dew.

Lord, I pray for your grace and perseverance this night.

(June 10, 2009)

Based on Joan's writing, here is a prompt on perseverance:

What do you struggle with? What can help you persevere through that difficult experience? Write about a challenging time. Then, imagine yourself on a journey. You get the spiritual help you need. Write about what will help you and transport yourself to a place that makes you feel easy and healed. Complete your writing with a prayer for perseverance.

Fear

I thought that as a result of my going to Lourdes, I banished fear. It is true that I feel peace and calm and acceptance and do not feel the fear reaction that causes my chest to squeeze and my stomach to flip and nearly paralyzes me. That went away during the trip to Lourdes.

When I look deeply, however, I recognize that I do have some fears. I fear not being able to breathe easily. That is why I decided to have a drain inserted into my left pleural cavity. But I fear the procedure and pain afterwards. That makes me anxious and tense. I realize that I have to relax more to prepare for it: listen to the Peggy Huddleston tape on preparing for surgery with visualization and relaxation. It is an antidote for the fear, and I will utilize it. I fear deep pain, which is why I take a Vicodin at night when my ear is hurting deeply. I fear lymph nodes that have popped up and the chest wall worsening. What will I do about it? Will Dr. Bar give me a chemotherapy that will help, or will he say there is nothing more he can suggest? Thinking about that fear makes me anxious. I know an antidote for that anxiety is deep breathing—yoga breathing and especially Tai Chi. I will incorporate the Tai Chi movements into my daily routine. It is necessary, just as I know the chair yoga exercises are necessary for leg mobility, and they are part of my daily routine. I fear for Chris fasting for four days. I was able to tell him that; he reassured me, and now I have to let it go.

I have to trust in God—pray and trust in God, and have faith that God will give me strength to go on as long as I can, and the knowledge and acceptance when it is time to let go. I am grateful to be celebrating our wedding anniversary of 43 years on August 6. I don't think we'll make it to 50, but one never knows.

May trust, faith, and love surround me tonight. May God hold me close and grant me a deep and healing sleep.

(July 24, 2009)

Based on Joan's writing, here is a writing prompt on fear:

What are the things you deeply fear? Write them out, and then for each one, write an antidote. What resources and tools do you have to combat your fear? Deep breathing, routine, friends and family, faith? What can you turn to in order to lessen your fear? Write about fear and end with a prayer for yourself.

Original watercolor by Joan M. O'Brien, 2009

Forgiveness

When Katherine Silvan was doing Reiki on me on Thursday, I had this thought about forgiveness. Are there resentments or grudges that I carry deep in my heart that must be released? I have actively released so much, but there are a few remnants that hopefully can be banished by putting pen to paper and expressing them.

The key one is my father. We never had a loving relationship in my mind, although he supported me in so many ways. I know my mother wanted to keep trying to have another baby, and she said he was not cooperating. I realize now that it was probably because of her health and all her miscarriages.

My mother took care of Uncle John's child, Kathy, while her mother was in the hospital. One day, my mother had to go out, and he was taking care of both of us. She was in the crib, and I was playing near her. She started crying. My father came in and instead of asking me what the problem was (JP-style), he automatically blamed me. I was shocked and hurt to the core and felt completely rejected.

When I was pregnant with Alyssa, he was not feeling well. We brought him to New Brunswick, where we were living in student housing, took him to the doctor, and he was diagnosed with Hodgkin's disease. He entered the hospital in New Brunswick, started receiving chemotherapy, and we visited him every day. I remember my Aunt Catherine visiting him once, and then accused us of killing him because he looked so bad. He went into remission and stayed with us in our apartment for a while, then went back to his sister's house in Bayonne. What I did not know until after he died was that she told him if he wanted to live there, he would have to put all his Sunoco stock in her name, which he did. That, in my eyes, was a betrayal and a shock. Perhaps he thought he would change it back one day. He met a woman, Ruth, and became engaged to her. Perhaps he thought he would change it when he married her and moved out. But he had a recurrence, and they all called us to take care of him. He came to the hospital in New Brunswick and never left. July 20th was the 40th anniversary of his death, the day Neil Armstrong walked on the moon, and Alyssa was two months old. It is time to let go. I forgive you, Dad. You were a good father, and I offer you my love and acceptance. May we both now be at peace.

As for Aunt Catherine, I have let bygones be bygones. She took my inheritance, took the jewelry my grandmother left me, and took the gold coins my father gave me, but that is the type of person she was, and I no longer harbor any anger for her.

(July 31, 2009)

Based on Joan's writing, here is a writing prompt on forgiveness:

Whom do you need to forgive? Write about that person or those people. Explain what happened and how you might try to see things differently now. Write about the hurt, resentment, and anger leaving your body. Write about letting your pain go and accepting peace into your life. Write about forgiveness.

Original watercolor by Joan M. O'Brien, 2009

Love

From Corinthians 12 a popular reading is the one on love: love is patient, love is kind, and so on. In the celebration of Agape at Emmaus, we talk of the different kinds of love: romantic love, agape love. I think of agape love as unconditional love. Unconditional love is usually directed from oneself to another person: a spouse, a child, a grandchild, a treasured friend. I realize tonight that I also have to direct unconditional love towards myself. This morning when I awoke after a good night's sleep, even with all the anticipation of Jen, Ariana, and Liam's visit and maybe because of it, I was feeling down. It's the same thing every day, the same dependence on others. I realize I was being too self-critical.

I need to unconditionally love myself for what I am, for surviving and thriving—I need to love my body for working hard. I need to love my mind for being able to write and read and process and interact with others. I need to love my soul for giving me grace and strength, faith, and hope, and the ability to give and receive love. It sounds so simple and easy. It should be, but it is not. I will meditate on love tonight, on loving myself unconditionally as well as giving and receiving love unconditionally from others. I pray that this realization will be my healing, my lifting up from any darkness or despair. I can't run around with my grandkids, but I can talk and interact with them. We worked on a puzzle together tonight and will again tomorrow.

I made a new commandment, a corollary to love your neighbor as yourself. It is love yourself as well as your neighbor. Amen to that.

(July 25, 2009)

Based on Joan's writing, here is a writing prompt on love:

Write about a favorite scripture passage. Try the one from Corinthians 12. What does love mean to you? What can you do to love yourself unconditionally? What does it mean to give and receive love? Write about love. End with a new commandment to help you heal.

Wisdom

Accept what is the reality of the moment and blossom with it.
When we moved back to France in 1982, I attended an orientation
workshop at the American Church in Paris called, "Bloom where you
are planted." That is the wisdom. Even with a bad stomach ache, I can
ride it out and figure out what I need to do to make it better. Number
one is rest, and I am so happy for this quiet, relaxing day. As I sit on
the porch on my lift chair, I am looking at the beautiful purple orchids
in front of me, lifting their heads to the sun, so happy to be in here, as I
am. My new prayer shawl is a beautiful purple like the orchids and
was crocheted by a woman in St. John's parish and delivered to Darien
High School for Michael to bring home to me. It is beautiful
handiwork and crocheted in the shape of a "V." The students at Darien
High School have been a loving and supportive community,
impressing me with their generosity and kindness to me and Michael,
sending flowers, raising money for the Bennett Cancer Center, and
sending many cards with personal messages to Michael expressing
their care and appreciation for him.

Number two on riding out the stomach ache is determining what food
would make it feel better this morning. Miso soup and toast and
Gaviscon were the right decision. Also analyze what may have caused
the problem and don't repeat that. Spicy soup for lunch, spicy shrimp
for dinner; overall, a lot of food eaten, my meds including Prednisone,
and a very busy day were all contributors. Today, I am in control of a
very bland diet and quiet day.

One concern I have had that is out of my control is spending ten hours
a day with a caregiver, day in and day out, while Michael is teaching.
He just said that Caroll may do it, which would be good since I know
her, and she knows my routine. Would she be able to take me to
doctors' visits and out for a ride once in a while? I know it will be a
period of adjustment, of planning each day, which I can control.

My wisdom as I reflect on this is to take it one day at a time, and enjoy
that day fully rather than looking at it as a long, dull period of time.
Time is a jewel to cherish, polish, and wear happily and gratefully. I
can read, I can write, exercise, watch my programs, have breakfast,
bathe, have lunch, nap, and the day will pass quickly. A friend may
visit now and then, and I'll speak with my children every day. It

sounds like a good plan. Alyssa mentioned working on the "Book of J" and writing my wisdom for the next generation. I like that. I also want to expand "The Quilt of My Life," which may be included in the "Book of J."

I like what Alyssa reminded me I told her when she was getting married: never go to bed angry, always look nice for your husband, and do something for yourself so you bring something exciting into the marriage. I will include that wisdom in the "Book of J."

(July 1, 2009)

Based on Joan's writing, here is a writing prompt on wisdom:

What life lessons do you have to share with others? What wisdom do you want to extend to future generations? Write about the wisdom you have from your experiences in life. Write about wisdom.

"Every human being faces that crossing over. I have much to prepare for that. I look forward to creating a legacy of words and love."

Church Music

Michael and I were discussing my funeral this morning for whenever the time comes. Best to be prepared. I am listening to music from St. Agnes, Will and Sarah's San Francisco church, on my iPod. I just love every song on that album. Oh, how nice it would be to have music like that. Then I think of what is available at St. Aloysius in New Canaan, and Ellen Sisson singing "Ave Maria" is nice.

How church music differs from church to church depending on the music minister. We are lucky at St. A's with ours. I remember the beautiful Taize adoration of the Cross and music during Lent ending our visit to Taize in France so many years ago. It imprinted a memory in our minds and hearts both visually and auditorally. I see the simple, austere chapel made holy by the reverence of people packed in the room—kneeling, praying, chanting—people of all faiths, bald-headed monks in brown robes, citizens in simple peasant garb from nearby villages, visitors from all over the world all kneeling in reverence or sitting on the austere wooden benches with backs, praying and chanting, a universal prayer of many faiths to one God.

From the serious and austere, there is the joyous church music associated with weddings. All the many chances for processing in and exiting after the vows have been professed. I remember listening over and over and helping Alyssa and Laird, then JP and Jen, and finally Will and Sarah, as they made their selections, each couple choosing different songs, expressing their personality. "Jesu, Joy of Man's Desiring" for walking in and "Trumpet Voluntary" for processing out are among the many selections.

Easter is always one of my favorites when I join in and sing "Jesus Christ has Risen Today, Alleluia," expressing renewal, rebirth, joy, and promise in the midst of white lilies, bells ringing out and chimes playing. Christmas is magic, a gift waiting to be opened and cherished. So many songs are poignantly beautiful—"Silent Night," "O, Little Town of Bethlehem," and "Angels We Have Heard on High." At weekly mass on Saturday night or Sunday, each mass offers its own musical menu. Soloists on Saturday evening and Sunday at 8 am, children's choir at 10 am, adult choir at 11:30 am, and teen group at 5:30 pm. Each one has its own allure and beauty.

Now my voice has dropped to a lower register, but once I was a soloist with a lovely soprano voice, singing in grade school, high school, and college, both at school and in the choir. Once I sang out freely and lovely. Now I listen and appreciate. I remember my years in the Ukrainian choir—"hos pu ti pu mil oy"—the somber, recusant sounds of the Byzantine music. As a yogini, I've listened to Buddhist chanting, not exactly church music, but peaceful and meditative in its own right. With all these forms, we give glory and celebrate life now or hereafter.

(May 23, 2009)

Based on Joan's writing, here is a prompt on church music:

What are your favorite religious songs? What memories do they evoke? Pick one of those memories and write about it. Then, write about your funeral— what music would you want? Happy and joyful or somber and serene? Write about church music.

Original watercolor by Joan M. O'Brien, 2008

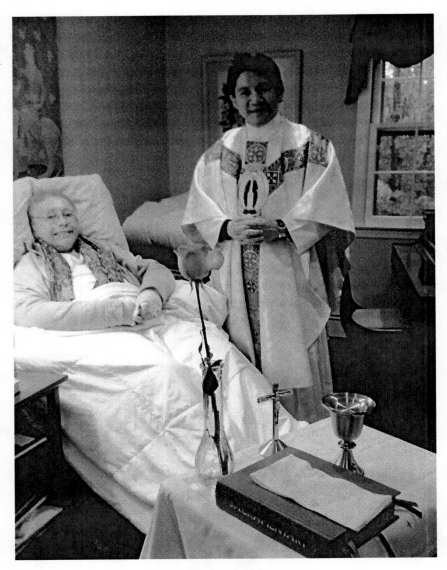

Joan with Father Ian, 2009

The Soul

Father Ian says that when the body dies, the soul lives. The soul is more than energy. It has intellect and free will—it is a perfect spirit.

I think of all the references we hear about the soul. "You are mine, body and soul," croons Frank Sinatra. "The soul magnifies the Lord," said Mary, when she agreed to be the Mother of God. We hear the terms "soul mate" and "soul music." I never attributed intellect and free will to the soul. I attributed it to the mind, but the mind is part of the soul.

How is my soul? I know it is better than it used to be because I am giving less attention to the beauty of the body. Not that I don't appreciate my body, for it has served me well for almost 67 years. I want to celebrate those 67 years and thank my body for all the feeling-good times: the exhilaration of running, of yoga, of pregnancy, of breastfeeding, of love, of wearing beautiful clothes, of travel to Europe, out to dinner, of cruising in Alaska, of travel to Colorado and California, of skiing in France, of dancing. My body was a gift of beauty.

I am not mad at you, body, for what you look like now. You endured mastectomy, chemotherapy, and radiation. You were a strong vessel enabling me to live fourteen years. You had such a strong immune system and still do, but the lymphatics are a challenge. The edema is a challenge. I just wish you could control it better. Can you try? My soul wants this too.

My soul, my intellect, is what will help me fly now, dance on the wet dewy grass, travel to Caneel Bay, visit exotic India, and walk the streets of New York City. My visualization and imagination will take me where the body can no longer easily go. Like a hummingbird, I will soar from flower to flower and above the trees, drinking the sweet nectar of a fluted flower.

(May 25, 2009)

Based on Joan's writing, here is a writing prompt on the soul:

What have you heard about the soul? What do you imagine the soul to be? Can you visualize how your soul will be—where it will go and what it will see—after your death? Write about the spirit; write about the soul.

Original watercolor by Joan M. O'Brien, 2009

Hour Glass

I allow the time to pass and
    accept gracefully the shifting sands.
I look and see what is presently before me as
    this moment is now and then done.

(September 15, 2008)

Based on Joan's writing, here is a writing prompt on time:

How can you accept the passing of time? Write about seeing each moment and letting it gently go. Write about your time on earth, writing about accepting when it is done.

"My writing is a tremendous means for me to express my feelings and emotions and innermost thoughts. I can truly say life is good."

CODA –
THE LAST CHAPTER

The Last Chapter

So many friends and family have showered me with love and kindness and generosity: visiting me, calling me, sending cards and flowers, bringing lunches and dinners. They are too numerous to mention every one by name but they include the parents of my children's spouses, my co-workers at Blair & Potts, my book group, my yoga friends, my Tai Chi friends, my Healing through Writing group, my WCA girlfriends, my women's group, my St. Aloysius community, my spiritual advisors Father Ian, Monsignor Cullen, and Monsignor Scheyd, my longtime friends from college and early married days, including the Cardaces, Hilgendorfs, and Beinsteins, the friends from living in France and those met over the years, especially Lynn, Tom and Kitty, and Holley, and my own angels, Maggie, Gina, and Sue.

My husband's eight siblings and their spouses who are as close as my own sisters and brothers would be. My special family, Erin and Lisa, my daughters-in-law, Jennifer and Sarah, and my son-in-law, Laird, as close to me as my children, and my children.

Chris is my eldest child and a talented musician. I admire his striving every day to become a person for himself and others. I am so proud of you, Chris, for all the changes have made and kept, for being a faithful son and a wonderful father to your son, Aidan. I love you so very much.

Alyssa, the second child, is my only daughter. We have become so close, almost thinking as one person. She nurtured me so much with a woman's tender loving care and a daughter's heart. Alyssa, I just love you so much.

Jean-Paul, also known as JP, was born in Paris and is my third child. From the time he was a very child, he was compassionate, empathetic, and kind to his family and to others. Now he is the loving husband to

228

Jennifer and father to Ariana and Liam. Thank you for everything, JP. I love you so very much.

Will, my fourth child, is my youngest, the baby of the family. He has grown into a leader, a director, a tower of strength for all of us. Give Will a request for information and it is researched on the Internet intently. He has a ready sense of humor, a contagious laugh, and is a loving son and plays beautiful piano pieces for us. Will, I give you much love to keep in your heart.

Michael, my husband, has been the love of my life for 43 years: a wonderful, kind, generous, supportive, and loving husband and father. He was always at my side, taking care of me, during my fourteen-year cancer journey. Michael and I met in graduate school when we were 23, fell in love, married a year later, and had our first child a year after that. Thank you, Michael, for your commitment, love, and support during our 43 years of marriage. I love you so passionately.

Finally, my grandchildren: Ariana, Aidan, and Liam. You are such a blessing and gift to me. I so loved every moment of our times together. I treasured them as jewels. Ariana, the first-born grandchild, my princess with whom I have always had a special bond, female to female. Aidan, vivacious, curious, sensitive with quite a sense of humor. Liam, with his ready smile, warm hug, and compassion for others. I would have liked to see you grow up, to continue to be part of your lives. To you and to my unborn grandchildren, I offer the following sonnet and desire that you carry me with you in your heart.

Ramage (Sonnet for my Descendants)

In you, my blood will flow through unborn years
and dreams that danced down all my days
will shimmer in yours; salt of my tears
your lips will taste. In many ways

I will be with you. Sparks from my fire
your lives will set ablaze; from me, the root,
what astral-blossomed boughs may yet aspire,
what ancient flavors hide in future fruit?

So I shall live, some part of me survive
in other minds, our kinship to proclaim.
Seeds of my visioning will someday thrive—
new music to old runes. The very Name
that in my heart now jubilantly sings
will lift your souls upon transcendent wings.

– Sister Marion Storjohann, SS.CC.

(September 11, 2009; read by Sue Lione at Joan's funeral mass)

JOAN M. O'BRIEN
June 5, 1942 –September 8, 2009

When my time comes
Let it come beautifully and peacefully
Let me be surrounded by my loved ones
My husband, my children
Holding my hands
All them together
Telling me I am loved

Walk with me gently
Through the day and night
Grant me sweet dreams and healing sleep
Until the dawn of a new day
— JMO

Joan M. O'Brien

Joan M. O'Brien, age 67, resident of New Canaan since 1985 and wife of Michael F. O'Brien, died at home on Tuesday, September 8, 2009, from breast cancer. She was first diagnosed in 1995.

Joan was born in Bayonne, New Jersey, on June 5, 1942, the only child of the late Joan and Martin Meehan.

She received a BS in chemistry from the College of Notre Dame on Staten Island, New York, and a MS from the Rutgers Institute of Microbiology, in New Jersey, with her thesis isolating and analyzing the structure of the antibiotic Gentamicin. During the first year of graduate school, she met and fell in love with Michael O'Brien, a mathematics graduate student. They were married in 1966 and had four children.

At the age of 50, Joan entered Pace Law School in White Plains, New York, where she was articles editor of the Pace Law Review. She received her Juris Doctor in 1995 at the same time that she was diagnosed with breast cancer, and she began a dual journey of fighting her cancer and following the law career she loved. She worked at the law firm of Blair & Potts in Stamford, Connecticut, for nine years.

Joan was an active member in the Emmaus Community of St. Aloysius Church. She loved to play tennis and travel, having lived in France with her family for eight years.

In addition, Joan was an artist and published writer. She displayed her oils, pastels, and watercolors at Silvermine and in New Canaan. She has written her reflections on life and has left these as a legacy for her descendants. She treasured and loved her family, friends, and medical team, and they in turn showered her with love and respect. She would like to be remembered for that love and for living in the moment and cherishing each day.

In addition to her husband, she is survived by her four children, Chris with his son Aidan O'Brien-Turner, Alyssa and her husband Laird Rawsthorne, Jean-Paul with his wife Jennifer and their children Ariana and Liam, and William with his wife Sarah.

(Obituary written by Joan M. O'Brien, edited by her family, September 2009)

GLOSSARY OF GRATITUDE

We offer this unconventional "glossary of gratitude" in the spirit of Joan's loving appreciation for all those who cared for her medically and spiritually, who brought her meals and communion, who made phone calls or trips to see her, who shared laughter and struggles, who worked, wrote, painted, prayed, and lived with her on her journey.

"I have a wonderful, wonderful family."

Joan's Immediate Family: Michael, Chris, Erin Love, Lisa Turner, Alyssa, Laird Rawsthorne, Jean-Paul, Jennifer, Will, Sarah, Ariana, Aidan, Liam.

Joan's Extended Family: Joan's parents Joan and Martin Meehan, her aunt Catherine Meehan, and those in Bayonne, New Jersey. Joan's family through marriage: Beatrice and Maurice O'Brien, and their nine children: Jim (and Kae), John (and Carol), Margie (and Arthur), Theresa, Michael, Vince (and Tina), Mary (and Peter), Patty, and Cathy O. Also Hans, Anne, Johan, and Adalynn Griesser; Tim (and Thuy) Griesser; Ken (and Isabel) Griesser; Christine, Mike (and Kim) and Ian Jones; Kevin (and Diane), Karen, Denis (and Allison) O'Brien; Michelle, Sean, Tommy, Mary Elizabeth and Rowan O'Brien; Jody, Daniel, and Michael Vincent O'Brien; Kelly (and John) Cairns; Bridget O'Brien; and all the extended family, including those in Ireland and those from Ireland living in America.

"Meeting a new doctor that you trust with your care is a positive situation… I must trust in my doctors and in my body's responses and in the guidance of my loved ones."

Joan's Medical Caregivers: Dr. Michael Bar, Dr. Steven Lo, Dr. Teresa Ponn, Dr. Frank Messino, Dr. Timothy Hall, Dr. Thau, Dr. Stepp, Dr. Bill Fessler, Dr. Maria Theodoulou, Dr. Jim

Talbot, and all the doctors over the years, along with their caring and expert staff, Joy Crowe, Ann Mundinger, Stamford Hospital, Yale Medical, Carl & Dorothy Bennett Cancer Center, Sloan Kettering, EMTs in California and Connecticut, Dr. Jerry Thrush, Dr. Nami, and the Genetech team.

"Every day I depend on the grace and strength from God. No doubt this help comes in the form of my wonderful caregivers, my husband and children, Caroll, Anita, and the others. What would I do without them?"

> **Joan's Hospice Nurses:** Caroll Morales, Pansy McNeil, Jean Meyer, Bonnie Vette, Alice, Anita, Cecilia, Minerva, Marita, Evina, Joy, and all those who helped in so many ways.

"I am grateful for all my caregivers. I am humbled. I am still smiling. I am still happy and hopeful. I am a flower—a pink flower, a rose, opening up its petals to the world."

> **Joan's Healing Team:** Rita Trieger and the Yoga Kula, Ken Dolan, Susan Weiss, and the Tai Chi class, Fran Becker, Vivienne Howell, Deb Pantolena, Amy Zabin, Katherine Silvan, Belleruth Naperstek, Bernie Siegel, Peggy Huddleston, Kripalu Yoga Center, all those at the Tully Center in Stamford Connecticut, Enso, Courtney Woodrow, the Kneaded Touch, Allura Wigs, Mr. Gu at Stamford Hospital, Jennifer Rokicki of Lymphatic Massage, Relay for Life, the Bennett Walks, Donnie Yancie, Elaine and Frank Harris.

"Nourish the virtues of faith, hope, and charity. Peter Cullen paid a surprise visit today, and Bill Scheyd comes tomorrow, and Ian on Sunday. My priest friends are looking after me."

> **Joan's Spiritual Team:** Father Ian Jeremiah, Monsignor Peter Cullen, Monsignor Bill Scheyd, Deacon John Tugman, the St. Aloysius Prayer Chain, Emmaus, Marion Glennon, Orly Benedict, the Knights and Dames of Malta, Rita Trieger and her Monks, the Lourdes team, Ellen Sisson, Father Tom Richstatter, Father Bill Eigel, spiritual communities in Marymount in

Neuilly, the American Church in Paris, St. Agnes in San Francisco, St. Thomas Aquinas University Parish in Boulder, the Sundance Lakota Indian spiritual community, St. John's Parish, St. Michael's in Greenwich, Life in the Spirit Seminar, prayer shawl knitters, communion bearers Gina Barber, Maggie Pierce, and Sue Lione, and all those praying or ministering to Joan.

"I found a new position in Stamford, Connecticut in a well-known estate planning law firm, Blair & Potts. I loved working there... I never worried about my cancer or a positive outcome with treatment because I was so fulfilled and happy with my work."

Joan's Law Friends: Nancy Blair, Arthur Potts, Bob Devellis, Sharon Blue, Kim Arpia, Gabby, Ellen, and all Joan's co-workers at Blair & Potts, the Blair & Potts team at the Bennett Cancer Center Walk, Janet Johnson, Joan's Pace Law School friends.

"Writing with friends and sharing is a best medicine... "

Joan's Fellow Writers: Sharon Bray, Drew Lamm, Rachel Simon, Joan Petardi, Antonia Gerard, Anne Bruhn, Fran Becker, John Tinker, Ken Nelson, Anne Morrow Lindberg, Bennett Cancer Center Writing through Healing Group, Stanford University Fallen Leaf Lake Write Retreat, Tom Barnes, Malena Watrous, Stanford Hospital Writing through Cancer Group.

"Painting a watercolor is very fulfilling, very engrossing. I can tune out the world and just concentrate on the mix to obtain the needed color, diluting it to obtain the proper intensity and then brushing it on the thick paper, and watch the magic of color and form give life."

Joan's Fellow Artists: Georgia Young, Bert DuAime, Kathy McCormick, Marie Cohen, Ann Dolorian, June Safford, Silvermine Guild Art Center, YMCA Artist Shows, Carl & Dorothy Bennett Cancer Center Artists.

"So many friends and family have showered me with love and kindness and generosity: visiting me, calling me, sending cards and flowers, bringing lunches and dinners.... There is so much beauty inside with all the flowers and love from family and friends. These are my blessings."

"Joan's Team" bearing food, flowers, cards, calls, company, and so much more: Sue and Jerry Lione, Gina and Al Barber, Maggie and Harrison Pierce, Susan and Gene Goodman, Susan and Jerry Reen, Merrily and Jim Krauser, Mary Lee and Bob McDougall, Terry Scarborough, Jennifer and Don Harrell, Audrey Spellman, Kitty and Tom Cross, Frank and Ellen McBrearity, Debbie and John Campbell, Lyn Bond, Mary and Rod Runstead, Kathy Pasternak, Paula Ryan, Penny and Dave Cattrell, Maureen Cozzi, Sue and David Scannell, Mary Aldrich, Val Maroney, Suzanne McGovern, Susie and Ernie Mysogland, Marianne Campbell, Lois Krippene, Lainy Krohley, Kathy and Paul Weaver, Kathy Garrison, Joy and Steve Sherry, Joanne and Bill Santulli, Holley and Gary Egloff, Judy and Jeff Boughrum, Carolyn and Tim Slipnicka, Mary Aldrich, Trudi Leddy, Ginger Novak, Jane Janis, Marylou Burke, Gale and Bob Stafford, Cindy Ording, Kathy Garrison, Debbie and Jeff Schumacher, Mary Ellen MacDonald, Lori Watson, Susan Weiss, Margaret and Brian Brady, Gail Banegan, Fran and John Koptiuch, Stephanie Scoon, Mary Jane and Neil Swanson, Barrie and Ralph Gonzalez, Cathy and Larry Wooters, Ceci and Jack Murray, Betsy Swanhaus, Frankie Stevens, and all those who showered her with blessings.

"What a gift to have such close friends whom you know love you and care for you so much, with whom I can be myself, not worry about how I look, and the real me can shine from inside to the outside."

Joan's friends from over the years: Barbara Matlosz, Lynn and Dominick Cardace, Pat and John Rose, Sabina and Len Beinstein, Gertrude and Alex Goldfinger, Lynn and John Fisher, Terri Bruce, Cynthia and Jack Harding, Elaine and Hal Abe, Maureen and Pat Grimes, Sue and Mike Hilgendorff, Jack and Barbara Manning, Felicia and Tony Santelli, Jordan and Jessica Boughrum, Inez Ferre, Carolyn Cross, Ada Osborne,

Julia and Jim Arliss, Dottie and Fred Wiele, Diane Cahill-O'Brien, Lynn Schoen, Charmaine Rawsthorne, Joe and Camille Taicner, John and Adeline Turner, Nancy Herman, Darien High School teachers, students, and staff, Dr. Carl Schaffner, friends from Fanwood, Katonah, Versailles, Paris, Neuilly, West Hurley, Wilton, New Canaan, California—Half Moon Bay, Stanford, Lake Tahoe—Colorado, and many more whom Joan held in her heart and now watches over with love.

"I am led down this happy, carefree path. I trust and I hope. I have faith in those I love."

Thank you for all your care, support, and love for Joan.

*Visit www.joansquilt.org for a multimedia showcase of Joan's legacy,
including photos, artwork, writings, and talks.*

LaVergne, TN USA
13 September 2010
196758LV00001B/33/P